Walter Dean Myers

by Elizabeth Hoover

SCHOOL OF EDUCATION
CURRICULUM LABORATORY
UM-DEARBORN

LUCENT BOOKS
A part of Gale, Cengage Learning

GALE
CENGAGE Learning·

Detroit • New York • San Francisco • New Haven, Conn • Waterville, Maine • London

GALE
CENGAGE Learning®

LIBRARY OF CONGRESS CATALOGING-IN-PUBLICATION DATA

Hoover, Elizabeth.
Walter Dean Myers / by Elizabeth Hoover.
    pages cm. -- (People in the News)
Includes bibliographical references and index.
ISBN 978-1-4205-0859-8 (hardcover)
1. Myers, Walter Dean, 1937---Juvenile literature. 2. Authors, American--20th century--Biography--Juvenile literature. 3. Young adult literature--Authorship--Juvenile literature. 4. African American authors--Biography--Juvenile literature. I. Title.
PS3563.Y48Z67 2014
813'.54--dc23
[B]
                                                                2013028450

Lucent Books
27500 Drake Rd.
Farmington Hills, MI 48331

ISBN-13: 978-1-4205-0859-8
ISBN-10: 1-4205-0859-8

Printed in the United States of America
1 2 3 4 5 6 7 17 16 15 14 13

Contents

Foreword   4

Introduction   6
One-Man Movement

Chapter 1   10
The Secret Joy of Books

Chapter 2   22
A Rocky Start to a Writing Career

Chapter 3   32
A Writer's Life

Chapter 4   44
Pain and Possibility on the Streets of Harlem

Chapter 5   55
From the Real to the Realer

Chapter 6   67
An Ambassador for Reading

Notes   78

Important Dates   84

For More Information   89

Index   92

Picture Credits   96

About the Author   96

Fame and celebrity are alluring. People are drawn to those who walk in fame's spotlight, whether they are known for great accomplishments or for notorious deeds. The lives of the famous pique public interest and attract attention, perhaps because their experiences seem in some ways so different from, yet in other ways so similar to, our own.

Newspapers, magazines, and television regularly capitalize on this fascination with celebrity by running profiles of famous people. For example, television programs such as *Entertainment Tonight* devote all their programming to stories about entertainment and entertainers. Magazines such as People fill their pages with stories of the private lives of famous people. Even newspapers, newsmagazines, and television news frequently delve into the lives of well-known personalities. Despite the number of articles and programs, few provide more than a superficial glimpse at their subjects.

Lucent's People in the News series offers young readers a deeper look into the lives of today's newsmakers, the influences that have shaped them, and the impact they have had in their fields of endeavor and on other people's lives. The subjects of the series hail from many disciplines and walks of life. They include authors, musicians, athletes, political leaders, entertainers, entrepreneurs, and others who have made a mark on modern life and who, in many cases, will continue to do so for years to come.

These biographies are more than factual chronicles. Each book emphasizes the contributions, accomplishments, or deeds that have brought fame or notoriety to the individual and shows how that person has influenced modern life. Authors portray their subjects in a realistic, unsentimental light. For example, Bill Gates—cofounder of the software giant Microsoft—has been instrumental in making personal computers the most vital tool of the modern age. Few dispute his business savvy, his perseverance, or his technical expertise, yet critics say he is ruthless in his dealings with competitors and driven more by his desire to maintain Microsoft's dominance in the computer industry than by an interest in furthering technology.

In these books, young readers will encounter inspiring stories about real people who achieved success despite enormous obstacles. Oprah Winfrey—one of the most powerful, most watched, and wealthiest women in television history—spent the first six years of her life in the care of her grandparents while her unwed mother sought work and a better life elsewhere. Her adolescence was colored by pregnancy at age fourteen, rape, and sexual abuse.

Each author documents and supports his or her work with an array of primary and secondary source quotations taken from diaries, letters, speeches, and interviews. All quotes are footnoted to show readers exactly how and where biographers derive their information and provide guidance for further research. The quotations enliven the text by giving readers eyewitness views of the life and accomplishments of each person covered in the People in the News series.

In addition, each book in the series includes photographs, annotated bibliographies, timelines, and comprehensive indexes. For both the casual reader and the student researcher, the People in the News series offers insight into the lives of today's newsmakers—people who shape the way we live, work, and play in the modern age.

One-Man Movement

In 1968 Walter Dean Myers published his first book, *Where Does the Day Go?* Written for children, it tells the story of an interracial group of kids who walk around the Harlem section of New York City trying to figure out what happens to the day when night comes. Today the book seems like a touching tale of childhood curiosity and imagination, but at the time it was a radical reinvention of what constitutes a children's book.

In the late 1960s, white writers who depicted white characters dominated the genre. Jim Naughton of the *Washington Post* called it "monochromatic." When Myers started publishing books that featured characters of color, this African American author became "a one-man movement,"[1] according to Naughton. Myers made visible the stories and experiences of African American children and teenagers and gave millions of young readers the chance to see themselves reflected in what they read.

At the time, not everyone was ready for children's books with black characters. When Myers penned his second children's book, *The Dragon Takes a Wife,* he created an African American fairy to guide a lonely dragon. Some readers were so incensed that he would dare to change the model of classic fairy tales that they sent him death threats.

Write What You Know

Despite the backlash, Myers did not want to write anything else. He has written more than seventy books for children and young adults, and the basis for all of them comes from his own experiences growing up in Harlem, the bustling center of African American life and culture during the 1950s and 1960s. While the neighborhood was plagued by crime, it was also a vibrant community and home to major black artistic figures, including the poet Langston Hughes.

Despite the fact that his foster mother was barely literate herself, she taught her son to read by reading to him from her *True Romance* magazines. The young boy fell in love with the sounds of words, and the shared activity of reading created a strong bond between the two. Myers experienced a rude awakening when he arrived at school, however. There he learned that the special language he shared with his mother was actually the result of her accommodating his near-debilitating speech impediment. His peers teased him ruthlessly about the way he talked, and he responded by hitting them.

He was labeled a troubled student and sent to the back of the classroom. And yet, a handful of teachers saw that this angry young man also had an aptitude and enthusiasm for reading and writing. They lent him books and praised his poems. Writing allowed him to communicate without being hindered by his speech problems, and reading books let him explore new ideas and possibilities.

A Secret Intellectual

As much as he loved reading, he kept it to himself, smuggling library books home in a paper bag so none of his friends knew. He was afraid they would tease him. As a boy on the cusp of manhood, he was supposed to prove himself by dunking basketballs or winning fights, not enjoying classics. Meanwhile his foster father never picked up a book or talked to Myers about writing.

As the end of high school approached, Myers realized his family could not afford to send him to college, and his book smarts no longer seemed to matter. Everywhere he looked he saw black men like himself pushing hand trucks, being garage attendants, or mopping floors. Meanwhile all the men he read about in books were white. "We exist in several worlds simultaneously," he wrote in an autobiographical essay. "As young people we hear that there is a world . . . [where] we are limited only by our willingness to work hard. . . . I began to suspect that was not true."[2] Instead he suspected his fate was sealed by his race, that no matter how hard he worked or how smart he was, he would still end up a laborer.

Reaching Troubled Teens

Like many African American teens, Myers became a high school dropout. After a stint in the army, he worked menial jobs. Eventually he found his way back into writing and—after a somewhat rocky start—established himself as a noted author. At first what drove him was the fact that he could dash off articles from his apartment without his editors knowing he was black. He did not face the kind of discrimination he encountered working in garment factories and at post offices.

What sustains him now is knowing he can change a young person's life with his writing. He can give his readers something he did not have much of as a teen: an opportunity to see himself and his community represented in an empowering and positive way. Referencing a scholar from the University of Chicago, Myers told National Public Radio, "What the text has to contain is some clue about this kid's humanity; some clue about that this book is OK for him to look at."[3]

Improbable Success

Over his more than forty-year career as a published author, Myers has amassed an impressive list of awards. He was even given a medal by the Library of Congress and named national ambassador for young people's literature.

This is all the more impressive given Myers had no role models growing up. "None of my acquaintances and no one in my family write," Myers recalls in his memoir, *Bad Boy*. "Yet I have become a professional writer. When I looked at what seemed at first a highly improbable circumstance, it all seems so amazingly logical. I am doing what I should be doing."[4]

In fact all the things that make his success seem so improbable—a barely literate mother, being a high school dropout, getting involved in petty crime as a youngster—are in fact what make him such a powerful writer. Because his experience is similar to that of his readers, he can create authentic representations of the world they know. All of his books feature characters on the brink of disaster—in lockup, about to pick up a gun, falling into drug addiction—that make decisions to change course or take responsibility for their actions.

Remaining Humble

Myers does not just hold a mirror up to the reality of urban life; he also tells teens that they have options and can take control of their lives even within difficult circumstances. This mix of urban realism and uplifting writing makes Myers a beloved and highly decorated author. He has much to brag about, but instead he concentrates on doing what he loves rather than relishing his awards. "I try not to make too much of my writing," he says. "My grandfather told stories, my father told stories, and that is what I do. Because I have published mine does not make me better than those who have gone before me."[5]

Nor does this giant in the field of children's literature believe his publishing record makes him better than those who will come after him. That is why he has dedicated his life not only to writing but also to being an educator, collaborator, mentor, and friend, nurturing the writing talents of high school students across the nation. After all, he writes not for professional accolades but to reach out to at-risk teenagers and pull them back from the brink before it is too late.

Chapter 1

The Secret Joy of Books

Growing up in a working-class family in Harlem, New York, during the 1950s, Walter Milton Myers thought that being a man meant working with your hands, playing sports, or battling it out on the streets with drug dealers. Many of the men in his life—his foster father, uncle, and neighbors—were not intellectuals; they were workers. Yet Walter was drawn to books and loved the escape they provided. While he may have had daydreams of being a writer, he did not imagine it was a real possibility for a poor black boy like him.

Working-Class Upbringing

Walter was born on August 12, 1937, in Martinsburg, West Virginia—one of seven children. According to Elizabeth Mehren of the *Los Angeles Times,* he was "a demographic disaster waiting to happen,"[6] meaning not much was expected for an African American boy living in rural poverty in West Virginia. When he was three years old, his mother died in childbirth, and his father—struggling with raising a growing brood of children—sent Walter to live with his first wife, Florence, and her husband, Herbert Julius Dean. The couple already had two teenage daughters, but they welcomed the boy as their own.

Herbert was African American, and Florence was part German and part Native American. At the time, their interracial relationship was a source of tension in the South so they moved to Harlem, a bustling African American neighborhood in New York City.

Romance and Ghosts

Walter's neighborhood may have been an exciting place, but the world right inside his apartment was also full of delights for a young boy falling in love with storytelling. Both his foster parents were barely literate, but Florence could read well enough to enjoy *True Romance* magazines and shared them with Walter, who fell in love with the sound of words. "The sound of Mama's voice in our sun-drenched Harlem kitchen was like a special kind of music, meant for only me," he remembered. "It was almost a secret language, one that only the two of us understood."[7]

Following along as Florence read to him, Walter quickly taught himself how to read, and the two switched roles. He read aloud to her as she did housework. They were very close—so close that the Deans' daughters teased him by saying he should marry Florence. He remembers following her around from room to room as she cleaned, knowing she would always listen to him.

He was not as close to Herbert, his foster father, a shipping clerk who often took on additional jobs to help make ends meet. But Walter does remember his impressive storytelling skills. Herbert Dean would entertain Walter with "endless stories," he remembers. "There were stories of ghosts and of rabbits that came through walls and of strange creatures that rose from the sea (the sea being the Hudson River.)"[8] Sometimes these stories were so scary to Walter that he had to ask Herbert to stop and remind him that he loved him.

Garbled Speech

The magic world of *True Romance,* ghost stories, and endless conversations was shattered as soon as Walter was old enough to go to school. At school he learned there was something wrong with him: He had a speech impediment. Walter heard the words he wanted to say clearly in his head, and he thought they sounded fine to him as he spoke; however, the teachers could not understand him and kept asking him to repeat himself, and the other students teased him by imitating his garbled speech.

"I arrived in school ready to conquer the world, but no one could understand a thing I was saying," he remembers. "That was very frustrating for me, and I responded by being angry."[9] He started to lash out, hitting kids who made fun of him. He was always getting into fights and even threw a book at a teacher. Florence was frequently called down to the school to deal with his misbehavior.

Finding Freedom in Books

It was hard for teachers to see that Walter had any talent or aptitude. His speech impediment meant he could barely read out loud, so teachers thought he was a poor reader. Because of his behavioral problems, he was dismissed as a problem student. A turning point came in the fifth grade. Fed up with his outbursts, his teacher sent him to the back of the room and told him he could no longer participate in class. He passed the time by reading comic books secretly, hiding them under his desk. When the teacher caught him, she tore his comics up. She told him if he was going to read he might as well read something worthwhile and gave him a collection of Norwegian fairy tales.

Walter thought it was the greatest thing to ever happen to him. He was enchanted by the book and asked to take it home. The teacher said he could not, but she would let him read it if he stopped causing trouble. Finally, she found something that could make Walter behave. She gave him a pile of classics, which he read at school. He also started working his way through the collection at the public library.

Reading offered him an escape from his clumsy, garbled speech. "Reading a book was not so much like entering a different world—it was like discovering a different language," he writes in his memoir, *Bad Boy*. "It was a language clearer than the one I spoke, and clearer than the one I heard around me. . . . The 'me' who read the books . . . seemed more real than the 'me' who played ball in the streets."[10]

By the age of eleven Myers had become a voracious reader of the classics.

A Gifted Student

That year, Walter received his best report card yet. In addition, his teacher had encouraged him to try writing down his thoughts as a way for him to communicate without encountering his speech impediment. His thoughts quickly became poems and stories. At the end of the fifth grade, the school magazine published one of his poems, and he ran all the way home with the magazine to show his mother.

In the sixth grade Walter received additional encouragement from a teacher, Irwin Lasher, a former U.S. Marine who had served in World War II. Lasher recognized talent in the youngster but also saw that Walter had serious confidence issues. Lasher spent the year trying to build Walter up, telling him he was smart. He also sent him to a speech therapist once a week. Lasher's pep talks worked: Walter decided he was smart enough to go college. He worked hard and was accepted into an accelerated program called Special Progress. When it came time for high school, he applied to and was admitted into the best public school in New York: Stuyvesant.

Myers applied to and was accepted at Stuyvesant High School, a prestigious public school in New York City, where he took his first creative-writing class.

"I Could Not Find Myself"

Walter started high school eager to learn and ready to take college preparatory classes. But he immediately encountered problems. Between his speech impediment and his shabby clothes, he was teased mercilessly by his peers and started skipping school to avoid their taunts. He became increasingly frustrated with his inability to articulate his ideas out loud and began lashing out—picking fights with students, teachers, and his foster parents. He struggled with math and science, subjects emphasized at Stuyvesant. Meanwhile he took his first creative-writing class and was praised for his ability. The contrast between the praise he received for writing and the dismal grades he got on his math tests was confusing and frustrating to him.

He loved reading the books his creative-writing teacher assigned him, but they did not make him think he could be a writer. None of the characters in the books or the authors who wrote them resembled him. It seemed that writing was something only rich white people could do. "I began a quiet devaluation of myself," he remembers. "I could not find myself in those books."[11] The books he read convinced him that his experience was not worthy of literature.

Troubles at Home

Shortly after Walter graduated from the sixth grade, his foster uncle Lee was beaten to death after being robbed outside a bar. Herbert Dean took his brother's death hard and retreated into a deep depression for over a year. This caused Florence to become distraught, and Walter felt her growing distant from him. He began to feel increasingly alone and isolated and responded by shutting the door to his room and burying his head in a book. The special relationship he had had with Florence evaporated in grief that year.

Later, in high school, Walter was shouldered with a greater financial responsibility. Herbert Dean's father went blind and had to move into their small Harlem apartment. This caused a financial strain, and Walter needed to start working to help out. He got a job at a garment factory, making fourteen dollars a week. He contributed five dollars a week to household expenses and kept four dollars for lunch, school supplies, and bus money. The rest Florence said she would hold on to so Walter could save up for a typewriter.

Later, when Walter asked her for the money, she tearfully confessed that she had spent it on lottery tickets. Walter was heartbroken, and the incident created more distance between them. Herbert was able to buy him a used typewriter—a big clunky thing that required him to hit the keys forcefully. The used typewriter was a bitter reminder of all that he could not have. "When the compromise comes, as it does early in Harlem to many children, it comes hard,"[12] he remarked.

Depression and Disillusionment

Nevertheless, he stubbornly pounded out stories on his typewriter but did not receive much encouragement from his family. Being a writer was not connected with success in his community. Success meant being a doctor, businessman, or other kind of professional. Walter decided to give up his dream of being a writer and achieve success by becoming a lawyer instead.

That dream was soon dashed as well. A family member scoffed at Walter's aspiration to practice law, telling him he did not speak well enough to be a lawyer. Pretty soon it became clear to Walter it did not matter if he could speak well enough—he was not going to college anyway. His family could not afford it. With college out of reach, going to school seemed less and less important, and he started to skip out more frequently.

While his classmates read college brochures after school, Walter worked in a garment factory. As he became increasingly aware of his family's poverty, he also started to understand that being black had consequences as well. Once he reached high school, his white friends started going to parties—parties he was not invited to because he was black. The guidance counselors at his school took the African American students aside and pointed out to them which colleges did not accept students of color.

One day, Walter was humiliated at work when he showed up only to discover a white boy had replaced him. He had been packing coats to be shipped, but now was demoted to pushing

The Harlem of the 1940s

Walter Dean Myers grew up in Harlem little more than a decade after the Harlem Renaissance, a period of intense musical, literary, and artistic growth in this growing African American community, centered around 135th Street in Manhattan. The growth of jazz clubs and African American–run publications ensured that Harlem remained a cultural heavyweight long after the Harlem Renaissance had run its course. By the 1940s, when Walter was in school, Harlem was still an epicenter of African American life and culture.

It was not uncommon for Harlem residents at the time to encounter jazz legends like Dizzy Gillespie and Billie Holiday walking the same streets as literary giants Countee Cullen and Langston Hughes. The neighborhood was also home to a number of prominent athletes and sports teams, including the famous New York Rens, the first all-black professional basketball team, and welterweight boxing legend Sugar Ray Robinson.

Most of Myers's memories of growing up in Harlem feature either basketball courts or churches. Churches in Harlem were more than a place of worship—they were also places where people could socialize and see performances by prominent poets and artists. "I remember Langston Hughes coming to read at church carrying a suitcase of his books to sell afterwards," Myers recalls. Myers grew up down the street from Hughes, a prominent writer known for his portrayals of black life and his experimentation with jazz poetry, heavily inspired by the music of the era.

Walter Dean Myers. "Walter Dean Myers: Memories of Harlem." *HarlemWorld*, March 3, 2008. http://harlemworldmag.com/2008/03/03/walter-dean-myers-memories-of-harlem.

Myers grew up in a Harlem that was the epicenter of African American culture.

hand trucks loaded with packages to the post office. He was hurt and frustrated because packing at least meant reading orders, but working the hand truck was nothing but manual labor.

College was already out of reach because of his financial situation, but the whole idea of college now seemed absurd to him anyway. All the jobs he saw African American men getting were menial ones, like factory worker or garage attendant. He did not see the point of working hard in school if he was going to end up pushing a hand truck. "I began to recognize that my 'rightful place' might be defined more by my race than [by] my abilities," he recalls. "I became depressed, disillusioned."[13]

Streets Versus Smarts

Walter hid his hurt through reading, skipping school for weeks at a time to climb a tree in Central Park where he would daydream. But reading felt like a secret activity, one he had to hide from friends and family. Reading was not considered "manly." Walter had always been big for his age, and by the time he was in high school, he was over 6 feet tall. He played basketball and baseball with his friends and read the sports pages avidly. He was praised for his athleticism, and a coach even floated the idea that he might be eligible for a basketball scholarship. Meanwhile, Walter secreted books home from the library in a paper bag to keep from being teased.

"There were two very distinct voices going on in my head," he remembers. "One had to do with sports, street life and establishing myself as a male. It was a fairly rough voice. . . . The other voice, the one I hid from my street friends and teammates was increasingly dealing with the vocabulary of literature."[14] Walter assumed that establishing himself as a male also meant getting into trouble. He and his friends started fights and played pranks. Once he and his friends sneaked into a bus terminal and tried to drive one of the buses. They were caught and had to go to the police station.

Frank

By the time he was fifteen, Walter had grown apart from his friends. His best friend growing up was white, and Walter could not go to the same parties as he. Also, all of his friends from his special accelerated class continued to do well in school, while he struggled. One day when Walter was walking to the park to shoot baskets, he saw a young man being beaten by three other men. Walter intervened, punching one of the attackers in the face. That gave the man being beaten a chance to fight back, and the three men ran off. The man Walter had saved introduced himself as Frank.

The two became friends, even though Frank was a few years older and was not much of a role model. Mostly what Frank did was drink. He also had a violent past. When he was in his early teens, Frank attacked a bus driver who was being rude to his mother and stabbed him to death, along with two other passengers. After serving time in jail, he had trouble getting a job and lived with his mother. Walter started hanging out with Frank until the early hours of the morning. Frank made deliveries for drug dealers, and Walter would tag along, splitting the money.

"Whatever Happens . . . "

Walter was adrift—hanging out with the heavy-drinking Frank, skipping school to read, and barely speaking to his foster parents. One day early in his senior year, Florence woke him up and said she was going down to school with him. Sitting in the guidance counselor's office, Walter watched teachers walk by. One of them was his English teacher. She crouched down to ask him if he was in trouble. He just shrugged. She told him, "Whatever happens . . . don't stop writing."[15]

The guidance counselor produced notes Walter had forged to excuse himself from school, and Florence was shocked. The counselor told them that Walter could stay in school only if he was supervised by a separate city agency and saw a therapist. Walter was now officially labeled a "troubled teen." At first, it seemed that he had turned a corner. He kept his therapist appointments and started attending school regularly. He even tried to limit his reading so he could concentrate on schoolwork.

The school's intervention came too late, however. Walter was already convinced that no matter what he did at this point, he

James Baldwin

Of all the books he read, Walter Dean Myers never saw himself in any of the characters until he read James Baldwin's *Sonny's Blues*. Baldwin was an African American novelist and essayist born and raised during the Harlem Renaissance. The oldest of nine children, Baldwin grew up in extreme poverty. Following in the footsteps of his father, Baldwin started a career as a preacher before moving to New York City's Greenwich Village to pursue writing.

Sonny's Blues, one of Baldwin's earliest short stories, tells the story of two brothers who grow up in Harlem following World War II. Sonny is a talented musician who becomes addicted to heroin at a young age. His older brother, a successful math teacher at an inner-city school, is responsible for looking out for Sonny, and he narrates the story. When Sonny's drug addiction lands him in jail, the two brothers experience a deep falling out. A family tragedy later in life brings them together again, and the narrator is there for Sonny when he is released from prison. He allows Sonny to stay in his house but worries about his brother's future. At the end of the story, Sonny invites his brother to watch him perform at a local jazz club. As he watches Sonny play the piano the narrator experiences a moment of revelation, struck by the way Sonny is able to transform his anger and suffering into an art of beauty and redemption.

Throughout his life Baldwin spoke candidly about the challenges facing African American writers in American society.

would not get anywhere in life. Pretty soon he started skipping school again, going to Central Park to read books by German philosopher Friedrich Nietzsche or Irish novelist James Joyce. The books made him ask questions about morality and life's significance, but he had no one to talk to about them. Meanwhile he kept filling notebooks with stories and observations about his neighborhood. He also spent more time with Frank, tagging

"Given the conditions in this country, to be a black writer was impossible,"[1] he said. "I knew I was black, of course, but I also knew I was smart. I didn't know how I would use my mind, or even if I could, but that was the only thing I had to use."[2] The themes of rage, race, imprisonment, and salvation in *Sonny's Blues* resonated deeply with many readers, including a young Myers, who had experienced segregation and racism.

1. Jordan Elgrably. "The Art of Fiction No. 78." Interview with James Baldwin. *Paris Review,* Spring 1984.

2. Quoted in American Masters. "James Baldwin." PBS, November 29, 2006. www.pbs.org/wnet/americanmasters /episodes/james-baldwin/about-the -author/59/.

The writings of James Baldwin (pictured) were an early influence on Myers.

along during drug deliveries. Sometimes these trips meant violent confrontations with other dealers or deliverymen.

It seemed that Walter had made his choice: He would reject school for life on the streets. However, the love of the written word that had started with his reading romance magazines to his foster mother as she ironed clothes would be tough to shake.

Chapter 2

A Rocky Start to a Writing Career

As he approached the end of high school, Walter Dean Myers was adrift, angry that his opportunities appeared so limited. His experience seemed to tell him that people like him could not be anything more than a laborer, but something kept drawing him back to reading and writing. Whatever that something was made it hard for him to accept the blue-collar jobs he perceived to be his fate. But he had no role models to show him how to build an alternative life. That, he would have to figure out on his own.

Locked Out

It was 1954 and the last few months of Myers's senior year of high school. He had not gone to school for weeks. Instead he forged notes that said his therapist wanted him to stay home. Out of school, he hung out with the heavy-drinking drifter named Frank or read in Central Park. Finally he got up the courage to take the bus down to Stuyvesant High School, but when he got there the doors were locked. A janitor told him the school year was over. Myers had missed graduation, although he had probably failed too many classes to graduate anyway. He wandered around the city for the rest of the day, not knowing what to do.

"I know what falling off a cliff means,"[16] Myers remarked about that moment. He could not bring himself to tell his parents. Instead he woke up every morning and left the house as if he were going to school. He would take a notebook and a book with him but neither read nor wrote. "The words on the page had stopped making sense," he explained. "Nothing I could write was adequate to express the despair I felt."[17]

Army Life

One day, he wandered into an army recruiting station and signed up. He was seventeen, just old enough to join. When he told his mother, she cried and asked him why he did it, but he did not have an answer for her. "I hadn't yet sorted out the shame I felt for having squandered my life. . . . Nor was I, with all my reading and writing skills, articulate enough to express my sense of being lost," he recalled. "What I did know was that I wanted to get away from home."[18]

Walter Dean Myers refers to his time in the military as "numbing years" during which he learned to kill efficiently and to teach others to kill efficiently but did not grow as a person.

The army allowed him to do just that—and not much else. At the time, the United States was not engaged in any conflict so Myers spent his days on army bases doing endless drills. He describes his three years as a soldier as "numbing years. Years of learning to kill efficiently. Years of teaching others to kill efficiently. Years of nongrowing."[19]

When he was not doing drills, he was playing basketball. Towering over most of the other players, he was the star of the team. During an important game, one of his superiors, a colonel, bet big on Myers's team's winning. When they lost, the colonel was so angry that he shipped the team off to the Arctic. It was hardly a punishment for Myers, however, as he had not seen much beyond Harlem and enjoyed the change of scenery. He loved the adventure, which reminded him of the writings of British poet Samuel Taylor Coleridge. Myers remembers, "I was surprised to find out that some of what I had considered to be merely fancy writing by Coleridge were actually fairly accurate descriptions of natural phenomena."[20]

Lost in Harlem

His three-year stint in the army gave him an adventure in the Arctic but did not prepare him for much else. When he was discharged at age twenty, Myers had no idea what he was going to do next. He moved back in with the Deans, who had relocated to Morristown, New Jersey, and got a job working in a factory. He hated his job, and he hated New Jersey.

He decided to move back to Harlem, where he rented a room that he shared with a growing family of cockroaches. He took a job at the post office unloading the mail chute and continued to write at night, but he had no idea what being a writer meant on a practical level. Instead he read memoirs by famous authors and tried to live in a similar way. That meant scraping by financially, keeping a notebook, and drinking.

Starting a Family

The starving-artist lifestyle may have been alluring to a young man with dreams of being a writer, but he discovered it was less appealing when he became a husband and father. In 1960 he married Joyce Smith, a caring and religious woman he had met at the post office, but Myers's lifestyle caused tension in their relationship. He stayed out late and could not hold down a job. After being fired from the post office, he jumped from job to job.

The couple had two children—Karen and Michael—but Myers found he still could not commit to the relationship any more than he could commit to a job. He continued to go out drinking and spend time with other women. The writing life kept calling to Myers, but more in style than in substance. He sported a beret like the other artists he saw and hung out in clubs with other writers. This frustrated Smith. "She was home with the babies and I was out with my bongos,"[21] Myers writes of that time, referencing a type of drum that was then popular with the artistic set.

Myers was not satisfied with his menial jobs. Writing gave him a sense of being something more than a laborer. It also was an activity that cost little—except for the fights it caused with his wife.

Color-Blind Writing

Being a writer was a romantic and exciting lifestyle choice, but after being fired from another job, Myers discovered it was also a way for him to make a little money. He started contributing articles to men's magazines, as well as to tabloids like the *National Enquirer*. It was not the kind of writing his heroes did, but he could make up to twenty dollars a story.

Writing also had another advantage: His editors did not know he was black, since he corresponded with them through the mail or talked to them over the phone. The discrimination he experienced at his other jobs, therefore, was not part of freelance writing. "I was facing absolutely no color line," he recalls. "Nobody knew who I was. I thought, 'I can do this stuff.' And I did."[22] Slowly he started to place articles in better publications.

Even though he was writing for more prestigious magazines, he was not completely satisfied. He was disheartened by how

The 1960s New York Literary Scene

New York City in the 1960s was in the throes of a mass counterculture movement. Artists, musicians, and writers were questioning mainstream culture and defying conventional modes of artistic production. Central to the spirit of rebellion and artistic experimentation was the Beat Generation, a group of young poets and writers who wrote honestly about their turbulent world. The term *Beat Generation* was coined by writer Jack Kerouac, who used it to refer to the way in which many artists and jazz musicians were "down and out, or poor and exhausted."

These artists flocked to bars and restaurants to share their ideas. The most prominent of these places was Max's Kansas City, where Beat poets rubbed shoulders with a new class of painters, sculptors, art critics, and musicians known collectively as the New York School. They shared a commitment to experimentation and rejected the art that directly preceded them.

Many African American artists and writers were excluded from the New York School by continued segregation, so some formed their own organizations, such as the Harlem Writers Guild founded by Myers's mentor, John O. Killens. The purpose of these organizations was to create a platform for young minority writers to present their work among peers that would understand their struggles.

Ann Charters. *The Portable Beat Reader.* New York: Penguin Classics, 2003, p. xvii.

Beat Generation artists, including writer Jack Kerouac (left, facing camera) and poet Allen Ginsberg (far right), meet at Max's Kansas City café.

little he earned and by the fact that he was writing mostly for a white audience. His opportunity to write for a more diverse group of readers came in the form of a contest sponsored by the Council on Interracial Books for Children, an organization that was trying to address the lack of diversity in children's literature.

Myers had never considered writing for children before, but he entered the contest anyway, not so much because he had a desire to write for children but just because he had a desire to write. His entry, titled *Where Does the Day Go?*, tells the story of a diverse group of children trying to figure out what happens to the day when night falls. The children discuss their theories with an African American father on a long walk.

Finding His Footing

Much to his surprise, Myers won the contest, and his book was published in 1969. Seeing his book in print, he realized he could do more than make money with his writing. He could also fill the void he experienced as a child: never encountering a character who looked or sounded like himself. He could write the kind of books that his own children could see themselves reflected in.

Myers had taken an important first step in establishing himself as the kind of writer he wanted to be, but he was still trying to find his footing. He was barely making ends meet as a freelancer, and his marriage was suffering. In 1970 he and Smith decided to divorce. Myers attributes the break to the stress incurred from his not having a steady income..

Myers moved to the Lower East Side of New York City and struggled to make a living as a writer. Around that time, he enrolled in a writing workshop at Columbia University taught by African American novelist John O. Killens. Like Myers, Killens had grown up in the working class and had done a stint in the army. Killens also cofounded the Harlem Writers Guild, a group of prestigious and prolific black writers.

Killens's own writing affirms and celebrates the experience of African Americans. For a budding black writer like Myers, whose early experience only exposed him to successful white writers,

Walter Dean Myers visits his old Harlem neighborhood. The publisher Bobbs-Merrill hired him as an editor and a recruiter and trainer of black writers.

Killens's workshop must have been a revelation. It introduced Myers to a community of successful African American writers united by a shared concern for promoting writing by African Americans.

Taking a Chance

Myers was single and broke, but he had a successful children's book under his belt. He knew he wanted to write books that would reach African American boys—boys like himself, who felt lost and invisible. Figuring out how to do that was his next challenge. Being a successful writer is a lot more than writing words on a page; it means understanding and participating in the publishing industry, something Myers knew nothing about.

He also continued to struggle with his speech impediment, which drained him of confidence. On the suggestion of a friend, Myers sought the help of a speech therapist. After working with the therapist, Myers could speak with greater confidence. But when his friend told him about a job as an editor at the Bobbs-

Merrill publishing house, Myers was reluctant to apply. "My friend accused me of being the kind of black person who is always complaining that he doesn't have a chance. Then when you give him a chance, he doesn't take it,"[23] Myers told the *Los Angeles Times*. His friend's words hit home, and Myers realized that he did not want to be that kind of person. Maybe this was the chance he needed. He decided to interview for the job.

Learning the Biz

At the time, publishing houses were eager to capitalize on the rising popularity of African American writing. Bobbs-Merrill wanted a black editor to help them recruit and retain black writers. Myers was offered the job almost immediately.

A section of the "Wall of Respect" in a Chicago neighborhood from 1967 until 1971 celebrates black literary figures, including (from left to right) W.E.B. DuBois, James Baldwin, Lerone Bennett, LeRoi Jones, Gwendoline Brooks, and John Killens, who was Myers's mentor.

Race in Children's Books

The Council on Interracial Books for Children was created in 1965 to address the need for more diverse characters in children's books. The council's initiative grew out of the civil rights movement of the 1960s, which drew attention to the social and political inequality faced by African Americans and other minority groups. As educators and policy makers reevaluated the laws that reinforced racism, sexism, and cultural stereotypes, it became clear that the textbooks used in children's classrooms perpetuated a negative and historically inaccurate view of women and people of color. One goal of the Council on Interracial Books, therefore, was to promote literature that reflected America's multiculturalism.

In 1968 the council established its annual writers' contest to encourage previously unpublished and underrepresented authors to contribute to the field. Walter Dean Myers's *Where Does the Day Go?* won the council's inaugural prize. Over the years, many of the manuscripts selected by the council were chosen for distribution by major publishing houses. By promoting writers of color and drawing attention to the subtle racism present in many American classics, the council worked hard to effect change in the American education system and to ensure that children were given the tools to turn harmful stereotypes into topics of discussion leading to deeper understanding.

The Council on Interracial Books for Children fought to overcome stereotypes of blacks, such as the "Aunt Jemima" stereotype pictured here, perpetuated in children's literature.

Surprised by this unexpected new development in his life, it took a while for Myers to get comfortable at his new post. On his first day, he was startled to discover that he had a large office and a white secretary. She kept popping her head into his office to ask whether he wanted anything, and he would always say no. Eventually he started asking her questions, and she filled him in as much as she could about the job.

He eventually became more comfortable on the job, which required him to find authors that he thought were talented and would sell. One of the things he did was take writers and their agents out to lunch to interest them in publishing with Bobbs-Merrill. He was astounded by how much money he was allowed to spend and the amount of food they would eat at those lunches.

Profit Over Art

The most important thing Myers learned on his new job was that publishing is a business concerned more with profit than with art. Decisions were driven mostly by how many copies the publishing house thought they could sell—not how good the author's writing was. He also saw how the salespeople marketed works by African American authors, thinking of them as a category separate from the rest of literature. "After the initial disillusionment about the artistic aspects of the job, I realized how foolish I had been in not learning, as a writer, about the business aspects of the craft,"[24] he reflects.

Even though he spent the day reading manuscript after manuscript, Myers still found the energy to do his own writing. Bobbs-Merrill published his second book for children, *The Dragon Takes a Wife*. His third, *The Dancers*, was published by Parents Magazine Press. Myers liked his children's books, but he also had an idea for a book for older readers. It was set on the streets of Harlem and featured young black men trying to find their way while surrounded by bad influences. It was the type of book that could have helped him find better options if he had read it as a teenager. Luckily he now had the connections, discipline, and knowledge to get that book into print.

Chapter 3

A Writer's Life

By the time he reached his midthirties, Walter Dean Myers had avoided the fate he thought was in store for him as a black man from Harlem. Instead of pushing a hand truck, he was an editor at a respected publishing house and a published author himself. With his knowledge of the book business and success as a children's book author, he was ready for the next phase of his career: that of an author of young-adult literature who represented the reality of urban teens from diverse backgrounds. To realize that next phase, however, he would need more than aspiration—he would need to cultivate the disciplined routine of a working writer and to get to know his readers as friends.

Settling Down

Just as Myers was ready to enter a new phase in his career, he was also ready to enter a new phase in his personal life. In 1973 he married Constance Brendel, an artist. He was determined to not make the same mistakes he had made with his first wife, but that did not mean he gave up all of his free-spirited ways. For example, he was playing the flute with a group of street musicians when he found out Brendel was pregnant with their first child, Christopher. It also did not mean that he turned his back on his first family, and he remained actively involved in the lives of Karen and Michael, his children from his marriage to Joyce Smith.

Myers also decided to change his name. He was born Walter Milton Myers, but he thought his name should reflect the fact that he was raised by his foster parents, the Deans. This became all the more important to him when his foster mother died in 1972. In 1974, he published his third children's book, *Fly, Jimmy, Fly!* under the name Walter Dean Myers.

A New Audience

In addition to changing his name, Myers was thinking about changing his audience: He wanted to write for young adults. He had an idea for a novel, but not yet a publisher. His agent, Harriet Wasserman, had secured publishing contracts for his children's books, and it was at a party she hosted that Myers found a publisher for his young-adult book.

Myers was not a big fan of parties and was uncomfortable in large groups of strangers However, he ended up engaging

Myers signs copies of his books for fans. In 1974 Myers changed his name from Walter Milton Myers to Walter Dean Myers to honor his foster parents.

Nikki Giovanni

When Myers was hired at Bobbs-Merrill, publishers were becoming interested in African American authors on the heels of the civil rights movement. The rise in African American literature in the 1960s was sparked by a new appreciation for black culture. Part of Myers's task was to bring in talented black writers to the publishing house. One of the first authors he signed was the poet Nikki Giovanni.

Giovanni was born in Knoxville, Tennessee, in 1943 and raised in Lincoln Heights, a predominantly African American suburb of Cincinnati, Ohio. She came from many generations of storytellers who encouraged her to pursue her passion. While at Fisk University, an all-black college in Nashville, she joined her peers in raising black consciousness through writing and civil rights activism. She was both the editor of Fisk's literary magazine and helped to reinstate the school's Student Non-Violent Coordinating Committee chapter, a group that played a significant role in the early civil rights movement.

After graduating from Fisk, Giovanni went on to Columbia University, where she met Myers in a writing workshop. Giovanni's first published works were politically charged and explored topics like the assassinations of civil rights leaders Malcolm X and Martin Luther King Jr. She was instantly hailed as one of the leading poets of the new black renaissance. Giovanni's poetry is strongly tied to methods of oral tradition in black culture and a sustained commitment to social issues.

Myers signed poet Nikki Giovanni to the Bobbs-Merrill stable of black writers.

in conversation with Linda Zuckerman, an editor at Viking, a large publishing house. She had read one of Myers's stories for children and enjoyed it so much that she agreed that night to publish Myers's first young-adult novel.

Joining the Good People Club

The novel, *Fast Sam, Cool Clyde, and Stuff,* tells the story of a twelve-year-old boy nicknamed Stuff who moves to Harlem. There he meets two slightly older boys named Sam and Clyde and a young woman named Gloria. The book centers on their friendship and how they help each other deal with difficult events like the death of Clyde's father. Together they form the Good People Club, a group that deliberately tries to do good and stays away from drugs and sex.

Published in 1975, the book was well received by critics and was named a notable book by the American Library Association. Reviewers lauded the fact that Myers's characters seemed like authentic teens to whom all readers could relate. He did this, he later said, by "humanizing the kid[s]. Giving the kids the same kinds of problems everyone else has."[25] In *Walter Dean Myers: A Literary Companion*, Mary Ellen Snodgrass dubs the characters in *Fast Sam, Cool Clyde, and Stuff* "anti-heroes," meaning characters who are not necessarily extraordinary, but who nonetheless do extraordinary things. She writes that the characters' "heroism arises less from valor than from spur-of-the-moment actions."[26] In other words, anyone can be a part of the Good People Club.

The characters in *Fast Sam, Cool Clyde, and Stuff* are able to make good choices and succeed not because they are especially gifted or talented (that is, heroic) but because they have each other. The book is informed by Myers's "belief that friendship can compensate for immaturity and wrongheadedness,"[27] according to Snodgrass. In this book Myers shows teens that they can resist the bad influences around them and rely on one another for support. Even though the book carries a serious message, Myers uses humor to engage his readers. Writing for *School Library Journal*, John F. Caviston notes, "The tone is alternately funny, sad, and sentimental, but it is always very natural and appealing."[28]

The Power of Friendship

Myers's positive message and approachable writing won him the support of librarians and teachers as well as legions of young readers. Following the success of *Fast Sam, Cool Clyde, and Stuff,* Viking offered Myers a contract for *Mojo and the Russians,* another book about a group of African American teens in Harlem. The book features a character who arranges marriages and who is based on one of Myers's aunts.

Like his previous book, *Mojo and the Russians* is sprinkled with humor and has an uplifting message about the power of friendship. Teachers appreciate the positive message, but young readers are also attracted to his books. Myers thinks the fact that his books feature teens in an urban setting and dealing with the realities of city life is part of their appeal. Myers suggested in an interview with the website Reading Rockets that that was because there were not that many books set in cities full of "brick buildings, fire hydrants, and fences. So many kids are attracted to that urban experience."[29]

A Voice for the Voiceless

While his young-adult books were doing well, Myers continued to pen stories for magazines, including an article on bullfighting that he researched while he and his family traveled in Peru in 1976. Shortly after they returned, however, Myers was fired from his job, in part because Bobbs-Merrill was restructuring, but also because the books by the black authors whom he recruited had not sold as well as the publisher had hoped.

Myers was devastated by the loss of his job and felt like somewhat of an outcast in the publishing world. To uplift his spirits, he took a trip with his wife and two-year-old son to Hong Kong and Thailand. On the plane he and his wife talked about the fact that they were lucky he had another book contract with Viking. What would happen, his wife asked, if, when they returned to New York, instead of looking for another job, Myers wrote full-time?

Traveling through Asia, Myers kept thinking about the suggestion. He considered whether there was a large enough market for black writers that he could make a suitable living by only writing. But something else was driving his decision making: the fact

In 1976, while vacationing in Peru, Myers wrote an article on bullfighting. Upon his return from that trip he was let go from his job at Bobbs-Merrill.

that there were hardly any books for children and young adults written for and about people of color. He knew he could help fill that gap; moreover, he felt he had a responsibility to do so, for "all the kids who are voiceless."[30] By the time Myers and his family got on the plane back to the United States, he had resolved to be a full-time writer and give a voice to those the publishing industry had ignored.

Writing as Life

By the time the family returned, Myers was nervous but ready to start writing full-time. Unlike when he was in his twenties, Myers knew that being a writer was more than a lifestyle choice; it meant making practical decisions about his career. For example, he knew he would have to publish not only novels but also stories and articles. He began to send out queries and to write for such publications as *Black World, Boys' Life, Parents,* and *Essence.* In addition, he tried different styles of writing, including nonfiction, mystery, and science fiction.

In 1976 Myers began writing full-time. To reduce living costs, he moved his family to Jersey City, New Jersey, shown here from the air.

He also knew he would have to find a new apartment that had enough space for both his family and an office. He wanted to stay in Harlem, the neighborhood that inspired him with its people and rhythms, but he also had to be mindful of not spending too much money. Realizing that the rent was high in the city, the family moved to Jersey City, New Jersey, right across the river.

Inspiration Everywhere

After settling in New Jersey, Myers started writing at an astonishing pace; he has published a book a year since 1977. In order to have such a prolific output, Myers must be inspired constantly. His wife, Constance, joked in an interview with the *Los Angeles Times* that she does not understand where all of his ideas come from. "Every two seconds or so, he'll say, 'Oh, I got an idea.' It's very annoying."[31] Often that inspiration comes when he is traveling to research articles or on vacation with his family. As he travels he asks himself what-if kinds of questions to prompt story ideas.

But he does not have to travel to exotic locales to get ideas. While he was searching for a new home for his family, for instance, he was struck by how many abandoned buildings there were in Harlem. He started to wonder what would happen if a group of teenagers took over one of those buildings. About three years later, Myers published *Young Landlords*, the tale of teens who take over a crumbling building in Harlem and find themselves in charge of a group of eccentric tenants. This book netted him his first Coretta Scott King Award, a prestigious award for writers of young-adult literature.

Myers also finds ideas for books by spending time with teenagers or simply walking around his old neighborhood. "Whatever bothers me becomes an idea for a book," Myers explains. "I go to juvenile detention centers and I see the young people in juvenile detention centers, so I write about those kids. Whatever I see inspires [me]. When I see things I like, . . . it becomes an idea for a book."[32]

Establishing a Writing Routine

With so many ideas for books, Myers had to develop a strict writing routine to keep up with all that inspires him. He gets up between 4:30 and 5:00 A.M. and begins working about two hours later.

Christopher loved the change in his dad's workday after Myers stopped leaving home to go to work at an office. "I would wake up in the morning, and there he would be," Christopher recalls. "And I'd go to sleep at night, and he would still be there. . . . His job was to make up stories, and I said, 'This is a great job. You do not have to go anywhere. You do not have to dress up fancy.'"[33] Even though Myers does not have to dress up, he still works hard. When he first started writing, he sat at his desk every day until he wrote at least ten pages. As he has gotten older, his pace has slowed, but he still writes around five pages a day.

The Prewriting Process

Part of the reason Myers can keep up such an impressive pace is because he meticulously plans all of his books. "I make a living by pre-writing. I'm a great pre-writer," he once quipped. He begins his prewriting by thinking deeply about his characters. He often starts by creating an entire time line for the character's life. "I need to know what this character might have encountered over the years,"[34] he explains, even if some of those things he puts on the time line do not make it into the book. The time he puts into thinking about all aspects of his characters pays off, as they are often what critics single out for praise.

When thinking about a character, he often pores over magazines or searches his own collection of historic photographs to find a picture that looks like what he imagines his character to look like. He also looks for photographs of places where his character could live or work. Then his wife makes an enormous collage of all the pictures that covers one whole wall of the room where he does his writing.

The next step is for him to outline his entire novel. He starts with an outline that he keeps developing until he sees that he has "a complete spectrum for a book. If it doesn't turn out, I destroy that idea,"[35] he says. He plots his book out scene by scene. This process, which can take a month, means that when it is finally time to write, he does not have to worry about the plot. Instead he is free to concentrate on the "colors and the fabric of the story."[36] Another upside of being such a careful planner, he says, is that he never gets writer's block.

A Meticulous Researcher

In addition to fleshing out his characters, Myers conducts in-depth research on every aspect of his books. This enables him to round out his stories with details that create believable settings and characters. After he writes his daily quota of pages, he usually spends the rest of the day doing research.

Often his research involves traveling, and, whenever possible, he brings his family along with him. In 1981 Myers published his first adventure book, *The Legend of Tarik*, set in North Africa during the eighth century. He researched the book while traveling in Morocco, where he learned about Islam. His travels to places such as Egypt, Peru, and the Czech Republic have also helped him write adventure tales packed with rich details.

Myers claims that the key to his large literary output is carefully planning his books. He notes, "I am a great pre-writer."

He also studies history for works such as the 2007 book *Harlem Summer*, which takes place in the 1920s. Myers read the major black newspaper of that era as well as other important black publications like the *Crisis*. He also did significant research for the 1994 novel *The Glory Field*, which tells the story of four generations of an African American family. The novel begins in 1753 with Muhammad Bilal, an eleven-year-old boy who is kidnapped from Africa to be sold into slavery in America. It ends in

Books for Children

Although he is best known for writing for young adults, Myers began his career by winning a contest for writing a children's book that featured diverse characters. After the publication of *Where Does the Day Go?* in 1969, Myers went on to write three other picture books: *The Dragon Takes a Wife, The Dancers,* and *Fly, Jimmy, Fly!*

Published by Bobbs-Merrill in 1972, *The Dragon Takes a Wife* tells the story of a lonely dragon who wins love. The book was significant for its inclusion of a strong, African American female character in the form of Mabel Mae Jones, the fairy who decides to take the dragon under her wing.

Parents Magazine Press published *The Dancers* in 1972. It is about Michael and Yvonne, two friends from very different backgrounds. Michael meets Yvonne when he goes to work with his father, a prop man for a ballet company. He invites her to visit his neighborhood and teaches her about life in a predominantly black community. In return, Yvonne introduces him to ballet.

Fly, Jimmy, Fly! is a prose-poem describing Jimmy's dream of flying like a bird over his inner-city neighborhood. Illustrated by Moneta Barrett and published by Putnam in 1974, it was one of Myers's first books to be distributed by a major publishing house.

1994 with the budding musical career of fifteen-year-old Malcolm Lewis. The generations in between keep passing along the leg irons that Bilal had worn as a way of acknowledging and honoring their past.

Myers's research is guided by a similar sense of the importance of history. His house in Jersey City is crammed with books and his historic photography collection, so he always has source material on hand.

Listening to Teens

After Myers finishes a draft of his novel, he asks for feedback on it from a number of people. First, Constance gives him comments, but because it is so important for Myers that his books resonate with teenagers, he also gets feedback from young people. As he got older, Christopher would read his dad's books and offer feedback as well. Sometimes Myers hires teenagers to read his manuscripts and tell him what they think. This method led him to realize that listening to teens was the best way to tailor his writing to their interests and needs. "One of the things that I really understand is that I want to expand their world," Myers once said. "But first I have to go into their world."[37] Their world was full of bullying, parents who are poor role models, crime, drugs, and violence. Myers knew that in order to reach these kids he would have to write about the dark and depressing aspects of their lives, but he also wanted to find a way to make his stories full of hope.

Chapter 4

Pain and Possibility on the Streets of Harlem

By the time he started writing his third young-adult novel, Walter Dean Myers had clarified his mission, and it remains to this day: to realistically depict the lives of black teens while at the same time furnishing his readers with examples of good decision making. To do that, Myers relies not only on his own life but also talks candidly to young adults about their experiences. With this material, he writes novels that unflinchingly depict the life and culture of the inner city. At the same time he shows his readers that their lives are not determined solely by their circumstances and that they can still make good choices even if they are surrounded by bad influences. This writing style has not only netted him millions of readers, but also a series of prestigious awards.

The Dark Side of Teenage Life

While his first two novels for young adults—*Fast Sam, Cool Clyde, and Stuff* and *Mojo and the Russians*—depicted urban life and featured black teenagers, they were mostly upbeat, positive, and full of humor. As he spent more time with teens on his neighborhood basketball court where he shot hoops with Christopher or in the twice-monthly writing workshops he taught in public schools, however, Myers wondered whether the lighthearted tone of his previous books was inappropriate for the readers he was trying to reach. After all, the students who took his creative-writing workshops did not write stories about "a teddy bear or their favorite Christmas," according to Myers. Instead, he heard stories "about a friend who is OD'ing [overdosing] on crack," or "about a girl who came home and her mother was on crack. She said she wanted to try crack, too."[38] Myers wanted to tell stories that would help these students imagine a different world for themselves and think about how they could avoid falling into a world of crime, violence, and drugs.

After he had taught inner-city teens and heard their stories, the tone of his novels started to shift. In 1978, he published *It Ain't All for Nothing*, a realistic novel about twelve-year-old Tippy. Tippy is being raised by his grandmother, a kind, religious woman who encourages him to live an upright life. When his grandmother gets too sick to care for him, Tippy goes to live with his dad, a jewelry thief. His dad seems uninterested in his son until he wants an accomplice for a robbery.

Myers signs books for teens. Teens like Myers's writings because he does not talk down to them and reaches them on their own level.

The tone of the novel is dark, and Myers writes poignantly about Tippy's loneliness and fear. According to critic Carmen Subryan, the novel "reflects much of the pain and anguish of ghetto life."[39] In her review of the book for the *Interracial Books for Children Bulletin,* Jane Pennington notes that Myers "pretties up nothing; not the language, not the circumstances, not the despair."[40] He took a risk by writing about urban reality—such depictions were rare in young-adult books at that time—but the risk paid off. The American Library Association awarded *It Ain't All for Nothing* the distinction of the best young-adult book of the year in 1978.

Gritty, Urban Realities

Myers continued to publish gritty, realistic portrayals of young, urban life. In 1979's *Young Landlords,* he tackles the issue of absentee landlords who preside over slum tenements and writes about a group of teens who try to rehabilitate one such building. In the 1981 *Hoops,* Myers describes the struggles of a seventeen-year-old basketball phenomenon from Harlem who hopes his ball playing can get him out of poverty. His coach warns him that as a person grows older, the "things you were dreaming about start to curl up and die."[41] In *Hoops,* Myers also tackles gambling, crime, and gun violence. His 1982 novel *Won't Know Until I Get There* tells the story of a juvenile delinquent who finds himself in foster care.

Julie Bosman of the *New York Times* writes that Myers tackles dangerous topics such as drugs, violence, and sexual experimentation as a way of challenging the resulting hopelessness and desperation that consume the lives of so many children. Myers does not write about crime and violence because he knows it will titillate readers. Instead he focuses on the toll that violence takes on families and children. Jennifer Brown, editor of *Shelf Awareness,* says that while Myers gives just enough details to depict such explicit themes, at the heart of these stories is "the emotional impact of the violence that these kids grow up around."[42]

In his 1981 novel Hoops, *Myers writes of a seventeen-year-old Harlem basketball phenomenon who hopes to use his ball-playing skills to escape from poverty.*

Seeing the Light in the Dark

"One of the things I want to do in my books is include a recognizable black community so that young people can at least see their community represented,"[43] Myers says about his realistic writing style. In order to do that, he populates his novels with characters like Tippy's abusive father but also the moral and gentle grandmother and a couple who tries to help the boy. Myers aims to capture the complexity of the African American community, instead of relying on stereotypes.

He also wants to offer students positive portrayals of characters of color. During a visit to a school in Brooklyn, he was surprised to hear a black student say he did not like to read books about African American characters. When Myers asked him why, the boy told him all those books were depressing and featured black characters that were either slaves or victims. Myers thought about all the books he knew about African Americans and realized how negative they were. "And then I thought," he told the *Los Angeles Times*, "'Well how can you avoid that and still write a realistic book?'"[44]

Myers's books appeal to teenage boys, a group that has had traditionally low levels of engagement with reading.

That is the challenge Myers takes on as a writer: to accurately portray the experiences of low-income African American teens who grow up in urban environments and yet also provide readers with positive images of black life. "He tackles difficult topics, but he does it in a way that is not without hope,"[45] Maria Salvadore, former coordinator of children's services for the District of Columbia Public Library, told the *Los Angeles Times*.

Reaching the Nonreader

Myers's emphasis on personal responsibility and making good choices has garnered him the support of teachers, libraries, and organizations that promote literature. He has won awards from the American Library Association, the Parents' Choice Foundation, and the Children's Books Council. His willingness to take on the subjects teens care about has netted him millions of readers. "He doesn't talk down to teens. He always reaches teens on their level,"[46] says Kimberly Patton, president of the Young Adult Library Services Center, explaining Myers's popularity.

One of the remarkable things about Myers's books is that they appeal to teenage boys, a demographic that has traditionally had low levels of engagement with reading. In terms of reading, they are the "toughest people to reach,"[47] according to Hillel Italie of the *Huffington Post*. And yet, many teen boys are drawn to his books. A sixth-grade student at the Harlem Children's Zone Promise Academy told Italie that Myers writes "about stuff I wanted to know, like basketball, what's going on in the street these days and how hard it is to get into college."[48]

But there is something more complicated going on with Myers's male characters than shooting hoops and hanging out on stoops. He artfully writes about the inner lives of boys in a way that acknowledges that they are complex characters wrestling with their identities. Roger Sutton, editor in chief of *Horn Book*, a publication about children's books, admires Myers's ability to tell these stories. He explains, "You see a sense of the interior life of boys and men, from a male perspective."[49]

Reading Can Make a Difference

Myers is driven by a belief that reading can make a real difference in people's lives. He dismisses the notion that books are simply an entertaining means of escape. "You can't do well in life if you don't read well,"[50] he told National Public Radio. He believes books teach young people important values and challenge them to examine their own lives. "Younger people gain a sense of control through self-exploration in most of his work,"[51] Salvadore explains. In other words, by seeing how Myers's characters struggle with their own circumstances, his readers realize that they too can take control of and be responsible for their own lives.

Working in juvenile detention facilities inspires Myers to write literature that will help young people see they are in control of their lives. He hopes his books will help juveniles as well as other people who are incarcerated understand how they ended up there. "They have to come to grips with the idea that they have responsibility for their own lives, no matter what . . . happens to them,"[52] he said in an interview with Learning First Alliance. Reading is an important part of the process of coming to grips with that idea. This belief pushes him not only to write but also to teach writing and reading in public schools and juvenile detention facilities.

The Shame of Illiteracy

Being raised by semiliterate caregivers, Myers saw how his foster parents were held back by their lack of education. His foster mother did her best to nurture her bookish son, although she had a hard time understanding him. His foster father, however, never praised or even read his son's writing. As a child, Myers was proud to show his mother a poem published in a school literary magazine, but his father just turned away. As Myers became a successful author, he sent copies of his books to his parents. "[My foster father] never said anything good about my writing," Myers says. "And that really, that really hurt, that really bothered me a lot."[53]

In 1986, Myers visited Herbert Dean in the hospital where he was dying of cancer. When he handed him a copy of his most

Fantasy and Science Fiction

While Walter Dean Myers is best known for his realistic portrayals of inner-city life, he is also the author of several adventure and science-fiction books. One is *The Legend of Tarik* (1981), about a young knight in Morocco who wants to avenge a family member's death. Tarik is initially driven by revenge, but through his quest he realizes the consequences of violence and decides to embrace peace.

The Righteous Revenge of Artemis Bonner (1992) also deals with revenge but in a more lighthearted setting. In the novel, Artemis Bonner sets out to avenge the murder of his uncle at the Bird Cage Saloon, located in the Wild West. He travels from New York City to Tombstone, Arizona, with the help of his sidekick, Frolic. While searching for his uncle's murderer, the two encounter treasure, adventure, and mishaps.

Shadow of the Red Moon (1995) tells the story of three friends, Jon, Kyraas, and Lin, who inhabit a primitive, Earthlike planet. At the start of the novel, they are forced to abandon their hometown, the Crystal City, in the middle of a war and a plague to search for their ancestral home, the Ancient Land. They are Okalians, a race of aliens, who are at war with the plague-ridden Fens. As they travel through the dangerous Wilderness to reach the Ancient Land, Jon, Kyraas, and Lin must overcome fear, racism, and violence to start a new civilization where Fens and Okalians live in peace together.

While each book has a fantastical setting, Myers incorporates elements of Harlem and inner-city culture, including struggles with violence and racism, as well as the healing power of friendship. His fantasy books highlight the absence of African American characters in traditional Western, gothic, and science-fiction genres by introducing strong black protagonists like Tarik and Artemis Bonner.

Myers began to promote literacy after realizing that his foster father had never read any of his books because he was illiterate.

recent book, Dean just put the manuscript down. After Dean died, Myers started going through family papers and saw that Dean had signed forms with the letter *X*. Myers then realized that his foster father could not read. "It tore me up," Myers said about that discovery. "I mean, I could have read him a story at the hospital. . . . But he was ashamed of the fact that he could not read. And that was a barrier between us all my life."[54] Even though his foster father was not actively engaged in Myers's writing, Myers still acknowledges him in interviews as a major influence—even without being able to write, his father was a gifted storyteller.

A Father-Son Collaboration

In 1984, after years of taking classes in the evening or between writing sessions, Myers graduated from Empire State College with a degree in communication. In addition to fulfilling a deferred

Christopher Myers

While Walter Dean Myers gave his son Christopher his first job as the illustrator for *Shadow of the Red Moon,* the younger Myers has gone on to accomplish many projects of his own. Christopher Myers first fell in love with art as a child, when his parents brought home photographs from flea markets. He went on to study at Brown University and honed his art while attending the Whitney Museum of Art's prestigious Independent Studio program. In an interview with the Reading Rockets website, Christopher described his illustrations as telling stories "about my neighborhood; about where I come from; about where I grew up" as well as describing "black people in ways that [I] want to see black people talked about."

Between 1999 and 2001, Christopher wrote and illustrated three books of his own: *Black Cat, Wings,* and *Fly!* Inspired by Christopher's own experiences growing up in and living in New York City, each book explores topics of friendship, creativity, and inner-city life. In addition to writing his own picture books, the younger Myers has also illustrated and interpreted works by important writers such as Harlem Renaissance novelist Zora Neale Hurston. Myers's photography, sculpture, and mixed-media artworks have been exhibited at the Studio Museum in Harlem, the Institute of Contemporary Art in Philadelphia, and the P.S.1 Contemporary Art Center in Queens, New York. Like his stories and illustrations, his artwork touches on topics of African American identity and race in an effort to restore humanity to those in need.

Quoted in "ReadingRockets. "Interview with Christopher Myers," April 19, 2012. www.readingrockets.org/books/interviews/myersc/transcript/.

Walter Dean Myers and his son Christopher. Christopher has been illustrating his father's books since 1995.

dream from his youth, finishing college also freed up time for him to coach Christopher's Little League Baseball team. He also remained an active part of the lives of his children from his first marriage. He dedicated his 1982 novel *Won't Know Until I Get There* to all three of his children.

As Christopher grew older, it became clear that he was a talented artist and enjoyed drawing. His parents encouraged him to develop his gifts, and he practiced drawing daily. After attending Brown University, he returned to New York and established himself as a talented illustrator of children's books. Being back in New York also gave him the opportunity to collaborate with his father.

In 1995, he contributed ten ink drawings to *Shadow of the Red Moon*, a fantasy novel by Myers. Two years later, they worked on *Harlem*, a children's book that celebrated the life and culture of that storied neighborhood. The younger Myers's vivid collages, ink drawings, and gouache paintings—the latter made of opaque pigments mixed with water and a gluey substance—were praised for their sense of color and movement. These illustrations and the elder Myers's text tell a different tale of Harlem than the one that appeared in *It Ain't All for Nothing* or *Young Landlords*. *Harlem* is about what made the neighborhood "a magical place," as Myers called it in his memoir, *Bad Boy*. He describes it as "alive with music that spilled onto the busy streets from tenement windows and full of colors and smells that made my heart beat faster."[55]

Working with his son has pushed the author to experiment with his writing. "He challenges me to reestablish and refine that passion within myself," the elder Myers says about working with his son. "So he's revived me."[56] In *Monster*, Myers experimented with a type of collage himself; he combined a fictional diary of a young man on trial for murder with portions of a screenplay. The younger Myers contributed haunting black-and-white images to go with the text.

By the time Myers wrote *Monster* in 1999, he was already considered a major figure in young-adult literature and had revolutionized the genre by featuring African American characters that defy stereotypes. While some of his realism garnered criticism, he would see his later books on war and crime banned outright by some school districts and libraries.

Chapter 5

From the Real to the Realer

As a writer, Walter Dean Myers is not limited to just one genre: He writes fiction, nonfiction, and poetry. A common thread throughout his books is the desire to accurately portray the lives of African American men and boys struggling with important life choices in hostile environments, including on the battlefield and in prison. His straightforward and frank discussion of these struggles has earned him accolades but also criticism. Some of his books have even been banned in certain schools and libraries for their controversial subject matter.

War Stories

On May 7, 1968, Myers's twenty-year-old brother, Sonny, was killed in a firefight in Vietnam after being in combat only two days. Myers was heartbroken and guilt-stricken. He worried that he had set the example for his younger brother by having joined the army himself. Sonny's death haunted him for years. In 1982 he traveled to Washington, D.C., with son Christopher to make a rubbing of Sonny's name from the Vietnam Veterans Memorial.

He also spent time researching the Vietnam War, learning about battles and interviewing veterans. Traveling to Thailand, which shares a peninsula with Vietnam in Southeast Asia and has similar geography, gave him a sense of the country's terrain. All that research came together in his 1988 novel *Fallen Angels*, a book that follows Richie Perry, an African American private as

Myers's brother Sonny was killed in Vietnam in 1968. As many others have done, Myers traveled to Washington, D.C., to make a rubbing of his brother's name on the Vietnam Veterans Memorial wall.

he experiences the horrors of the Vietnam War (1955–1975). Myers dedicated the novel to Sonny.

When Is Real Too Real?

Fallen Angels shows the disturbing and terrifying aspects of war and depicts how soldiers' judgments can be clouded both by fear and by the army rhetoric meant to dehumanize the enemy. Myers does not spare his readers the gory aspects of battle. There are scenes of enemy soldiers cutting ears from corpses and American servicemen firing on innocent civilians. At one point, Richie describes a Vietnamese woman blown to bits by the booby trap she is trying to deliver to his platoon. "I saw part of her body move in one direction, and her legs in another,"[57] he says.

The book is still considered groundbreaking in young-adult fiction for its realistic depiction of war. Critic Mary Ellen Snodgrass calls *Fallen Angels* Myers's "masterwork."[58] Writing for *School Library Journal*, Maria Salvadore describes the book as "compelling, graphic, necessarily gruesome and wholly plausible."[59] The book earned Myers his third Coretta Scott King Award, his second Parents' Choice Award, and his fifth American Library Association's Best Book for Young Adults designation.

Not everyone, however, appreciates the book's graphic nature. Shortly after it was published, various schools and libraries banned it from their shelves for its edgy subject matter. It has been dropped from school curricula in Ohio, Kansas, and Texas. In 2003, a group called Parents Against Bad Books in Schools tried to get it removed from school libraries in Fairfax, Virginia, because of its "profanity and descriptions of drug abuse, sexually explicit conduct, and torture."[60] The school district held firm, however, and the book remained on the shelves. "I think it's silly," Myers says about his books' being banned and challenged. "People don't understand that by withholding information from people, you hurt them. You're not protecting them."[61]

Shortly after its publication, Myers's Fallen Angels *was banned from various schools and libraries because of its controversial subject matter and depictions of the brutality of war.*

Sportswriting

One of the major themes across Walter Dean Myers's many novels is the relationship between teens and sports. As he notes in his memoir, *Bad Boy*, Myers had many identities growing up, one of them being a neighborhood basketball star. His books on sports often deal with the promise of athletic success and the tensions that arise from balancing sports, relationships, and academics.

Hoops, Myers's first young-adult sports novel, was published by Delacorte in 1981. The protagonist, Lonnie Jackson, trains to compete in the citywide basketball Tournament of Champions. When a crisis of conscience arises on the eve of the big game, Lonnie must learn to push aside all outside pressures and make a difficult decision on behalf of himself and his team.

Published in 2008, *Game* also tells the story of an inner-city teen with dreams of earning a college scholarship and playing for the National Basketball Association (NBA). Drew Larson is a talented basketball player who struggles against an overbearing coach, a tough and unforgiving neighborhood, and his own pride and ambition. Leonard Marcus of the *New York Times* called Drew's ability to gain perspective on his experiences as perhaps "childhood's hardest lesson."

Leonard S. Marcus. "Boys to Men." *New York Times*, May 11, 2008. www.nytimes.com /2008/05/11/books/review/Marcus-t.html?pagewanted=all.

In 2012 Myers served as honorary chair for the annual children's art auction at BookExpo America, with proceeds supporting the Kids' Right to Read Project and American Booksellers Foundation for Free Expression (ABFFE). Prior to the event, Myers stated, "Over the years, I've seen censorship grow. The bottom line is that the America we love needs our support. We have to stand up and be counted."[62]

From Vietnam to Iraq

Like his father and uncle, Michael Myers, the author's eldest son, joined the armed forces. As a member of the U.S. Air Force, he served in the Persian Gulf War (1990–1991) in Iraq. When the

United States invaded Iraq for a second time in 2003, Myers decided to take on the moral ambiguities of that war. In his 2008 *Sunrise Over Fallujah,* Richie Perry's nephew Robin "Birdy" Perry joins the army despite his family's objections and is shipped out to Fallujah, a city in Iraq.

Birdy believes in the righteousness of the war and is sure the conflict will bring democracy to the region. Once in Iraq, he experiences a rude awakening. He watches the body count rise, both of his friends and of the civilians they are meant to protect. He thinks the Iraqis will greet him and his fellow soldiers as liberators, but they instead seem suspicious and hostile. Birdy starts to wonder whether winning the war is even possible.

The *New York Times* called *Sunrise Over Fallujah* an "astonishing book."[63] In the journal *Kliatt,* Paula Rohrlick writes, "This somber novel will help anyone trying to understand the war and the experiences of our military there."[64] While these and other critics praised the book for its sensitive portrayal of a soldier's struggle, various groups objected to its ambivalence about the Iraq War. *Sunrise Over Fallujah* joined its predecessor *Fallen Angels* on banned-books lists across the country.

Prison Writing

Troubling current events like the Vietnam and Iraq Wars prompt Myers to research so he better understands not only the background and history of the event but also how it affects those involved. Another issue that troubles Myers is the rising incarceration rates in the United States. The United States has the developed world's highest incarceration rate and is home to nearly a quarter of the world's prisoners, despite having just 5 percent of the world's population. There are 751 people in prison for every 100,000 Americans. In comparison, Russia, which has the next highest rate, has 627 prisoners for every 100,000 people; England has 151; and Japan has 63. Incarceration is a hot-button political issue with complex moral, social, economic, and policy concerns.

In the 1980s, Myers started researching the lives of prisoners and their experiences in jail. He formed a lifelong interest in the

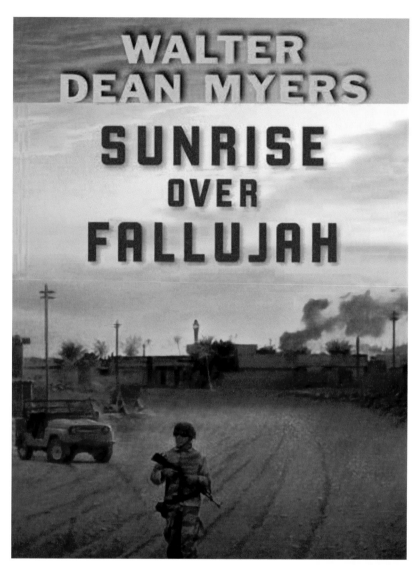

Praised by both critics and students, Myers's novel Sunrise Over Fallujah *was still placed on many banned-books lists across the country.*

criminal justice system. This interest began in 1983 when he was prompted by a class at Empire State College to interview adults who had been or currently were in prison. Over two months' time he accumulated more than five hundred pages of interviews with prostitutes, drug dealers, and even murderers. "I was fascinated by how similar my background was to some of the prisoners with whom I talked,"[65] Myers writes in an autobiographical essay.

Given their similar backgrounds, Myers could not help wondering how they had ended up behind bars while he had ended up a successful writer. "I had acquired the strength to turn away from disaster. Sometimes the turning away was a last minute decision, but nevertheless it worked,"[66] he concluded. He wondered whether his writing could help these individuals develop that strength and make sense of the choices that had landed them in jail.

Spending Time in Juvenile Detention

Many of the people he interviewed had children who were also incarcerated. Myers wondered whether he could intervene so that they did not spend the rest of their lives in jail like their parents. To reach out to these young people, he started working in juvenile detention centers as a visiting writer. One thing he noticed is that juvenile offenders had countless opportunities to "turn away from disaster," yet did not take them. "I talked to defense attorneys and prosecutors, and they all said the same thing: that no one starts off as a murderer," says Myers. "They all start with small crimes and work their way up."[67]

At some point between dropping out of school and shooting someone during a robbery, the teenager could have made a different choice and taken a better path. Yet none of the people he worked with in jail thought like that. "These guys were like jailhouse lawyers, so to speak," he says. "They knew the law backward and forward, but there was no moral discussion."[68] They were able to distance themselves from their actions, thinking of them in terms of legal technicalities instead of actual consequences. Myers remembers meeting a young convict who was so far removed from his crimes that he talked about them in the third person.

Making a Monster

Although he wants the teens he works with to make better choices, Myers also acknowledges that there are societal influences that contribute to juvenile crime. In his 1994 acceptance speech for the Margaret A. Edwards Award for his contributions to young-adult literature, he castigated American society for its "silent assent" to the "destruction"[69] of teenagers. In his 1999 novel *Monster* he exposes the institutional indifference to the plight of juveniles through the story of sixteen-year-old Steve Harmon, who awaits trial for murder at the Manhattan Detention Center. At night, Steve tries to keep his sobs quiet as he listens to young prisoners being beaten.

In the novel, Myers also depicts the kind of distancing he saw among juvenile offenders. Steve is an aspiring filmmaker, and the book consists of his diary entries and film scripts. He tells his story at a distance—from behind his imaginary camera. In Myers's experimental style of collaging the diary entries and script, the reader is never sure of Steve's innocence or guilt. A reviewer for *Horn Book* writes that Myers "adeptly allows each character to speak of him or herself, leaving readers to judge for themselves the truthfulness of the defendants, witnesses, lawyers, and, most compelling, Steve himself."[70]

Many think that Myers's 1999 novel Monster, *about a teenage boy on trial for murder, is the peak achievement of his career.*

For Myers, Steve's actual guilt—as determined by a court of law—is not the point of the novel. In his diary, Steve asks the kind of moral questions that Myers found troublingly absent in the conversations he heard in lockup. Critics praised Myers's creation of a compelling and unique narrative voice, something the book shares with young-adult classics such as J.D. Salinger's *Catcher in the Rye* and S.E. Hinton's *The Outsiders*. Critic Patty Campbell writes that *Monster* "joins these landmark books. Looking backward, *Monster* is the peak achievement of a career."[71]

Bullies Make More Bullies

Like many of the people Myers encountered in prisons, Steve lived under the constant threat of violence and intimidation. He is bullied by older boys in his neighborhood and goaded into joining them when they decide to rob a store. Most of the offenders Myers works with in juvenile facilities have been bullied most of their lives and pressured by older teens or even adults to commit crimes. In turn, they become bullies themselves.

He takes on the topic of bullying more fully in *Shooter*, a book that tells the story of a school shooting through newspaper clippings and interviews. Published in 2004, the book was inspired by the 1999 school shooting at Columbine High School in Colorado. After the shooting, Myers traveled to Columbine to speak to students. "What I saw was kids being bullied," Myers explains to the educational website Scholastic. "[They were] pushed around, sometimes by fellow students, sometimes by family members. These kids would get so angry and upset. I saw kids being bullied, and I saw them reacting to being bullied."[72]

Like the students he saw being bullied, the two characters in *Shooter* are forced to navigate a dangerous and hostile high school environment. In their frustration, they turn to violence. "I think that the problem with so many young people is that violence gets to be a resource," Myers explains in an interview with Hazel Rochman. "When nothing else works for you, violence always does."[73] He hopes his books will show teens who are being bullied that they are not alone and that they should seek help before reaching for a gun.

Making History Come Alive

Part of the reason Myers's fiction is so vivid is because he researches every detail of the subjects he writes about. In other words, he brings nonfiction's commitment to accuracy to his fiction. Meanwhile, Myers's nonfiction is enlivened with novelistic storytelling techniques. He has written a number of biographies of important African Americans as well as chronicles of the Vietnam War and the 1839 Amistad affair, in which African slaves revolted and took over a British ship.

Just as Myers creates full and complex characters for his novels, he also makes historical figures come alive on the page. In reviewing Myers's 1991 history text *Now Is Your Time! The African American Struggle for Freedom*, Michael Didra of the *Washington Post* declares that Myers writes with "the vividness of a novelist, the balance of a historian and the passion of an advocate. He tells a familiar story and shocks us with it all over again."[74] Myers enlivens this work on African American history with portraits of historical figures such as Prince, a slave owned by Thomas Jefferson, and journalist Ida B. Wells. In addition, he weaves in his own family's story, including that of his great-grandmother, who was a slave.

In his full-length biographies of people such as the black leader Malcolm X and the Haitian revolutionary Toussaint L'Ouverture, Myers strives to write in such a way that his subjects seem like human begins rather than static icons entombed in time. In his 1993 *Malcolm X: By Any Means Necessary,* he focuses on Malcolm X's evolution from a petty criminal into a powerful leader. In addition, he challenges other historians' depiction of Malcolm X as violent and hateful. His 2001 biography of the boxer Muhammad Ali, *The Greatest*, garnered praise from critics who lauded this affectionate portrait of a sports icon. Writing for *Booklist*, reviewer Bill Ott opined: "This is finally a story about a black man of tremendous courage. The kind of universal story that needs a writer as talented as Myers to retell it for every generation."[75]

Malcolm X and Muhammad Ali are well-known figures, but Myers brought equal attention to his biography of an unknown West African princess who was rescued from a sacrificial death by a British sea captain and brought to England in 1850. Myers

In his biographies of people such as Malcolm X (pictured), Myers shows his subjects as human rather than larger-than-life figures entombed in time.

pieced together this remarkable story from letters and newspaper clippings he discovered in a used bookstore in England. The resulting book, *At Her Majesty's Request: An African Princess in Victorian England,* tells the story of the girl's friendship with Queen Victoria. A reviewer for *Publishers Weekly* praised the book as a "moving and very human portrait of the princess."[76]

Bad Boy

Perhaps Myers's most moving portrait is the one he drew of himself. His 2001 memoir, *Bad Boy,* concentrates on his early life and ends shortly after he joins the army at age seventeen. In this work, Myers writes frankly about the struggles he experienced as a black teen in Harlem and how he struggled with depression as he tried to find his path. Although he was writing about his own life, he still approached this project with his typical thorough researching process. He looked at census records and listened to oral history from his family members.

Columbine

Walter Dean Myers's *Shooter* was partially inspired by the events that took place on April 20, 1999, at Columbine High School in Littleton, Colorado. On that morning, two high school seniors, Eric Harris and Dylan Klebold, entered their school carrying firearms and explosives. In less than an hour, the two gunmen had killed thirteen classmates and teachers and wounded twenty-four more before eventually committing suicide. The Columbine shooting was branded the deadliest school shooting of its time and the first to play out on live television.

The events at Columbine transfixed the nation and raised questions about adolescent depression, violence, and bullying. In its aftermath, new policies on bullying and gun control were put in place in schools nationwide. Schools began initiating zero-tolerance policies against threats and weapon use. Restrictive gun control laws requiring child safety locks on all newly produced handguns and banning the import of high-capacity ammunition clips cited Columbine as a preventive example. Most telling of all, the FBI convened a summit in Leesburg, Virginia, three months after the attack to assemble a psychological profile of the killers and shed light on the phenomenon of bullying and school shooters.

The Columbine memorial was dedicated on September 21, 2007, at Clement Park in Littleton to remember those who were lost in the tragedy.

One of the more dramatic aspects of the book is the contrast between the struggling "bad boy" protagonist and the "about the author" on the book's back cover that lists Myers's many accomplishments. As he approached his seventies, Myers had become one of the most decorated young-adult writers of all time. His honors recognized him not only for his writing but also for his advocacy of literature and literacy—a task Myers gladly shoulders with or without the accolades.

Chapter 6

An Ambassador for Reading

By the time he reached the age of seventy, Walter Dean Myers had penned more than seventy books and had won some fifty awards and honors. These include some of the most prestigious awards available to American authors, such as a National Endowment for the Arts grant, a Newbery Honor, and a Margaret A. Edwards Award for lifetime achievement. In 2012 he was named national ambassador for young people's literature, a position created by the Library of Congress and the literacy advocacy group Every Child a Reader. To mark the occasion, the Library of Congress held a ceremony in which they presented Myers with a medal. His task as ambassador is to promote reading and literacy among young adults. But Myers has been an "unofficial" ambassador for reading since he authored his first book in 1968.

Visions of Reading

In his novels, Myers makes a subtle but powerful case for reading by representing it as both transformative and pleasurable. In *Fallen Angels* a young character stays up past lights-out reading comic books under the covers with a flashlight. In *The Outside Shot* a woman reads to the protagonist to help him recover from a drinking binge. In *Handbook for Boys: A Novel,* patrons of the neighborhood barbershop try to convince a boy to read by telling him it will help him be successful in business. One character says, "Being in America is like having a box of tools I can use to build any kind of life I want."[77] One of those tools is reading.

In his essay "And Then I Read . . . ," Myers writes about how reading gave him a sense of freedom when he was a boy: "In my imagination I could also be a participant in adventures that were beyond the limits of the self."[78] Myers depicts such freeing experiences with reading in his fiction. For example in *The Beast*, a character describes sharing works of literature with his girlfriend in Central Park: "I'd become suddenly heroic, had been able to fly, to

Professional basketball player Kevin Martin reads to second-grade students as part of the Read to Achieve program. Myers frequently participates in the program by visiting schools and libraries to talk to students about his works.

soar over the familiar gray of the city."[79] Myers's protagonist is lifted up by language—even language that he does not quite understand.

Opening Doors to Reading

In an effort to share this experience, Myers writes novels that are both accessible and exciting to populations who have low levels of engagement with reading. Because of this, librarians and educators often choose his books when they organize events to promote reading. It does not hurt that Myers is also willing to visit schools and libraries to talk to students about the works. In addition, he is also a frequent participant in the National Basketball Association's Read to Achieve Program.

Visiting schools is not the only way Myers helps to make his work accessible. In 2009 he helped create the Second Chance Initiative, a program that uses his novel *Dope Sick* to help students learn to make good choices. (In the book, a young man who is involved in a drug deal that goes bad has an opportunity to go back in time and make better choices.) As part of the initiative, the book was made available online for free. In addition, AdLit.org, an organization that supports teachers and parents who work with struggling readers, distributed study guides, lesson plans, and activity ideas to go along with the book.

Pushing the Genre Forward

In addition to promoting reading, Myers is a trailblazer in young-adult literature. His daring style and subject matter have changed the genre and opened doors for a diverse group of writers who want to write for young adults with various backgrounds. He challenges notions of what is appropriate for this age group. He has also proven that experimental narrative techniques like the collage style he used in *Monster* can be understood and appreciated by young people.

While critics have suggested his work is too adult, he thinks teens deserve and appreciate challenging work. At the 2001 National Book Festival sponsored by then First Lady Laura Bush, Myers defended his writing. He said, "I've been accused of writing adult books and calling them 'Young Adult' books. Where does one stop and the other begin?"[80]

Beloved by Teens

For Myers, there is no reason not to write young-adult books about "adult" subjects like violence, drugs, crime, and sex, especially since many teens living in urban and even suburban environments have already been exposed to these issues. As a boy, Myers encountered gangs, dealt with the challenges of being a foster child, and watched his friends experiment with drugs. Because of this, he can write authentically about those experiences. In turn, young readers feel a deep connection to Myers's characters and to Myers himself.

In 2002 students in Detroit were asked to vote for an author they wanted to come speak to them at the city's Author Day. Overwhelmingly, they chose Myers. Ruth Birsdorth, the event's chairperson, had one word to describe the author, "Wow." She added, "He is a librarian's dream come true. He writes for all ages and interests and finds something that everybody can identify with. He is a brilliant author."[81]

Myers receives a steady stream of fan mail from readers who recognize themselves in his characters. He thinks that is the main reason why readers identify with his writing. "They hear names and circumstances that are familiar things, so the book becomes a friendly place to be,"[82] the author says.

From Fan Mail to Manuscript

Myers tries to respond to fan letters as often as he can and sometimes develops meaningful relationships with the people who write to him. One such relationship grew into a collaboration. In 2008, he received a letter from thirteen-year-old Ross Workman, a student from New Jersey who had long admired Myers's work. Myers wrote back and asked the boy whether he would like to write a book together.

Ross immediately replied yes. "I did not even have to think about it," Ross said. "This invitation from Walter Dean Myers— my favorite author—was too good to pass up! If I had thought

Myers's writing workshops for kids are one way he has made his work more accessible to young readers.

about it, I would have worried more about whether I could actually write a book."[83] It turns out that Ross could indeed write a book. Four years later, they published *Kick*, a novel about a troubled teen who finds direction in playing soccer.

Myers has also been a mentor to some of his fans who are aspiring writers. In 2010 Myers corresponded with an inmate of a North Carolina prison. The thirty-year-old convict wrote to Myers and said he wanted to be a writer. Myers responded by mailing him books on writing. He also read the prisoner's novel, all two hundred handwritten pages of it.

Cultivating the Business

From fan mail to school visits and even collaborations, Myers has cultivated a special relationship with his readers.

This relationship helps him promote literature to reluctant readers. In addition Myers nurtures writers and publishers who are committed to writing and publishing books for and about African Americans.

In 2002 he participated in the Langston Hughes Children's Literature Festival, a celebration of this important African American poet. As a part of the festival, Myers and publisher HarperCollins launched the Walter Dean Myers Publishing Institute. The five-year project for undergraduate students was meant to make publishing accessible to a diversity of voices. This issue was so important to Myers that the author invested his own money in the endeavor, matching what HarperCollins gave.

Nurturing Writers

While growing up, Myers thought that being a writer was something out of reach, something that only white people could do. Part of his institute's mission is to show young people of color that being a writer is an attainable goal. "I do not think [writing] is something that very, very special people can do," Myers wrote in *Read* magazine. "It can be learned. It can be taught."[84] He knows this firsthand because he travels across the country teaching writing to diverse populations.

In addition to teaching in the schools and juvenile detention facilities near his home in Jersey City, he has traveled across the country to lead creative-writing workshops in schools. For example, he worked with students in Texas writing family histories and witnessed firsthand how writing can help students, even the ones who do not end up pursuing a writing career. Myers told a community radio station in Tampa, Florida, about a student who had written to him after the semester had ended. In the letter, the young man said that he did not know whether his writing had gotten any better, but he did know that his relationship with his family had. Myers explained, "I think that what they were learning was the use of language. How communicating on a more intense, more intimate level is useful."[85]

Prison Writing Workshops

In addition to leading workshops and literacy initiatives in secondary schools and universities, Walter Dean Myers has spent extensive time as a visiting writer and workshop leader in prisons and juvenile detention centers. Because his work often deals with crime, broken family lives, and growing up in tough urban environments, it strikes a chord with the personal struggles of many inmates.

In his workshops, Myers encourages young writers to embrace their cultural heritage, to claim personal responsibility for their actions and livelihoods, and to express themselves, using his own life as an example. "When I tell kids about my background," he says, "the reaction is very often 'If you can do this . . . if you have gone through these things, then I can also.'" His stated goal is to teach kids to think about what their lives are about in the most basic sense. "I have enormous faith in young people," he says, when describing his experiences working with inmates. "I think if we challenge them more and if we give them a clearer idea of what life expects from them . . . I don't think we're giving them a clear idea. . . . We have to say [to them], 'This is up to you.'"

Quoted in Learning First Alliance. "Prophet of Second Chances: A Conversation with Acclaimed Author Walter Dean Myers." *Public School Insights* (blog), January 31, 2009. www.learningfirst.org/node/2319.

Myers's prison writing workshops have been successful because inmates can relate to the subjects in his books.

Rescuing Teens

By promoting reading and writing, Myers believes he can empower teenagers to make better decisions, communicate more clearly about their experiences, and take responsibility for their actions. However, he knows they cannot succeed on their own. He also believes that society has an obligation to help young people not only survive but thrive. In a 2009 interview with the Learning First Alliance, he spoke about the astonishing dropout rates among African American high school students: "As far as I'm concerned, from a national point of view as an American, we have to rescue these kids. We have to reverse this. We have to go into these communities and turn this around."[86]

In his public appearances, interviews, and published articles and editorials, he urges communities to allocate more resources to education. When the federal government spent

In public appearances, interviews, and published editorials and articles Myers promotes the allocation of more resources for education.

Banned!

Walter Dean Myers's challenging subject matter has created tensions in schools and among special-interest groups. Of the seventy books that he has published over the last four decades, three have consistently been banned somewhere and thus have appeared on the American Library Association's Banned Books List.

In 2001, both *Hoops* and *Fallen Angels* were challenged in separate school districts. Parents in Vanlue, Ohio, pressured the school to remove *Hoops* from an English class reading list because of its profanity, derogatory language, and sexual content. The school refused, and the book remained on the class list. Parents challenged *Fallen Angels* in Arlington, Texas, because they felt that the content was unsuitable for young readers. It has since been banned in school districts in Georgia, Kansas, and Indiana.

In April 2009, Judi Wheelan of Iowa's Council Bluffs School District urged school officials to ban *Hoops* from county classrooms and libraries after her sons brought it home from elementary school. School officials, aided by the Kids' Right to Read Project, voted unanimously to keep it in district libraries. In 2012, parents of the Blue Valley School District in Kansas unsuccessfully petitioned for *Monster*'s removal from classrooms for "vulgar language, sexual explicitness, [and] violent imagery that is gratuitously employed."

American Booksellers Foundation for Free Expression. "Banned Books Week Handbook: The Stories Behind Some Banned and Challenged Works," May 3, 2012. www.abffe.org/?page=BBWStoriesBehind.

hundreds of millions of dollars to bail out struggling banks and automobile manufacturers in 2008, Myers penned a passionate editorial in the *Huffington Post* calling dropout rates "a national scandal." He asked, "Are we actually willing to pretend that the automobile industry is a greater resource than the youth of America?"[87]

Myers believes that fathers can make a big difference in their children's lives just by reading to them for thirty minutes a day.

"A Bold Choice"

Throughout his career, Myers has advocated on behalf of teens as well as worked to empower young people to make their lives better. Because of his commitment to young adults, he was named ambassador for young people's literature by the Children's Book Council in 2012. When asked what he wanted to achieve in this post, he replied that he wanted to engage with low-income parents. He explains, "You take a black man who does not have a job, but you say to him, 'Look, you can make a difference in your child's life, just by reading to him for 30 minutes a day.'"[88]

His goal may seem modest, but Myers has seen how powerful the simple act of reading can be. When he was a boy, he spent time with his mother every day reading magazines. This simple act sparked a lifelong love of reading and started him on a path to becoming a successful author.

While his popularity with young readers makes him a natural fit for this position, Julie Bosman of the *New York Times* suggests that his appointment might be viewed as "a bold statement."[89] He is the first writer of color to be appointed to the post, and his work boldly confronts topics such as crime, drive-by shootings, poverty, and gangs. Executive director of the Children's Book Council Robin Adelson defended the council's selection of Myers by saying that the message at the core of these dark books is that anyone can achieve his goals if he believes in himself. She believes his appointment to the post also makes sense because of his versatility. His works offer "a little bit of everything," from a "deep knowledge of history" to a "definite hard-core, hard-edge realism."[90]

With Writing and Reading, Anything Is Possible

Critics may say that Myers's books are too dark for young people, but they reflect the world he knows and the world in which his readers live. He believes that ignoring the harsh reality of their lives will only turn them off to reading and make them feel invisible. Myers was able to use his experiences—for example, dropping out of high school, running errands for drug dealers, getting into fights—and sculpt them into a rich body of literature. He has arrived at a place he never thought possible when he was a high school dropout sitting in Central Park full of despair.

He is a decorated author who has traveled the world researching his books and enjoys a placid life in his home in Jersey City. There he writes in his upstairs office and takes breaks to play the flute. While his writing career has earned him respect and admiration, that is not his focus. Most important to him is that his work inspires others to believe they can also achieve their dreams, no matter what circumstances they find themselves in.

Introduction: One-Man Movement

1. Jim Naughton. "Literary Crusader Writes Stories About Real Kids." *Washington Post*, December 29, 1989, p. 8.
2. Quoted in *Something About the Author.* "Myers, Walter Dean." Autobiography Series. Vol. 18. Edited by Alan Hedblad. Detroit: Gale Research, 1994, p. 146.
3. Quoted in National Public Radio. "To Do Well in Life, You Have to 'Read Well.'" *Morning Edition*, January 10, 2012. www.npr.org/2012/01/10/144944598/to-do-well-in-life-you -have-to-read-well.
4. Walter Dean Myers. *Bad Boy*. New York: HarperCollins, 2001, p. 199.
5. Quoted in *Something About the Author.* "Myers, Walter Dean," p. 155.

Chapter 1: The Secret Joy of Books

6. Elizabeth Mehren. "Fountain of Stories for Youth." *Los Angeles Times*. October 15, 1997. http://articles.latimes .com/1997/oct/15/news/ls-42828.
7. Myers. *Bad Boy*, p. 14.
8. Quoted in *Something About the Author.* "Myers, Walter Dean."
9. Quoted in Teen Reads. "Biography: Walter Dean Myers." www.teenreads.com/authors/walter-dean-myers.
10. Myers. *Bad Boy*, p. 46.
11. Quoted in James M. Abraham. "'Harlem' Writer Myers Repays a Debt." *Sarasota (FL) Herald Tribune,* April 21, 2002, p. E4.
12. Quoted in *Something About the Author.* "Myers, Walter Dean," p. 147.
13. Quoted in *Something About the Author.* "Myers, Walter Dean," p. 146.
14. Myers. *Bad Boy*, p. 92.
15. Myers. *Bad Boy*, p. 153.

Chapter 2: A Rocky Start to a Writing Career

16. Quoted in Hillel Italie. "Walter Dean Myers, 73-Year-Old Author, Beloved by Young Readers." *Huffington Post*, March 5, 2012. www.huffingtonpost.com/2011/03/04/walter-dean-myers-author_n_831559.html.
17. Myers. *Bad Boy*, p. 188.
18. Myers. *Bad Boy*, p. 196.
19. Myers. *Bad Boy*, p. 200.
20. Myers. *Bad Boy*, p. 100.
21. Quoted in *Something About the Author*. "Myers, Walter Dean," p. 149.
22. Quoted in Mehren. "Fountain of Stories for Youth."
23. Quoted in Mehren. "Fountain of Stories for Youth."
24. Quoted in *Something About the Author*. "Myers, Walter Dean," p. 153.

Chapter 3: A Writer's Life

25. Quoted in Naughton. "Literary Crusader Writes Stories About Real Kids," p. 8.
26. Mary Ellen Snodgrass. *Walter Dean Myers: A Literary Companion*. Jefferson, NC: McFarland, 2006, p. 55.
27. Snodgrass. *Walter Dean Myers*, p. 55.
28. John F. Caviston. Review of *Fast Sam, Cool Clyde, and Stuff* by Walter Dean Myers. *School Library Journal*, March 1975.
29. Quoted in Reading Rockets. "Transcript of an interview with Walter Dean Myers." www.readingrockets.org/books/interviews/myersw/transcript/.
30. Quoted in Naughton. "Literary Crusader Writes Stories About Real Kids, p. 8.
31. Quoted in Mehren. "Fountain of Stories for Youth."
32. Quoted in Scholastic. "A Talk with Walter Dean Myers." http://teacher.scholastic.com/scholasticnews/indepth/bullying/bullying_news/myerstalk.htm.
33. Quoted in Reading Rockets. "Transcript of an Interview with Christopher Myers." www.readingrockets.org/books/interviews/myersc/transcript/.

34. Quoted in Adolescent Literacy. "Walter Dean Myers's Second Chance Initiative." www.adlit.org/second_chances/.
35. Quoted in Scholastic. "A Talk with Walter Dean Myers."
36. Quoted in Adolescent Literacy. "Walter Dean Myers's Second Chance Initiative."
37. Quoted in Learning First Alliance. "Prophet of Second Chances: A Conversation with Acclaimed Author Walter Dean Myers." *Public School Insights* (blog), January 31, 2009. www.learningfirst.org/node/2319.

Chapter 4: Pain and Possibility on the Streets of Harlem

38. Quoted in Naughton. "Literary Crusader Writes Stories About Real Kids," p. 8.
39. Carmen Subryan. "Walter Dean Myers." In *Afro-American Fiction Writers After 1955*, edited by Thadious M. Davis and Trudier Harris-Lopez, pp. 199–202. *Dictionary of Literary Biography*. Vol. 33. Detroit: Gale Research, 1984.
40. Jane Pennington. Review of *It Ain't All for Nothing* by Walter Dean Myers. *Interracial Book for Children Bulletin.* Vol. 10, 1979.
41. Walter Dean Myers. *Hoops*. New York: Delacorte, 1981, p. 40.
42. Quoted in Julie Bosman. "Children's Book Envoy Defines His Mission." *New York Times*, January 3, 2012. www.nytimes.com/2012/01/03/books/walter-dean-myers-ambassador-for-young-peoples-literature.html?_r=1&pagewanted=all.
43. Quoted in Jarrett Dapier. "Young Adult Realism." *In These Times,* May 9, 2011. www.inthesetimes.com/article/7283/young_adult_realism.
44. Quoted in Naughton. "Literary Crusader Writes Stories About Real Kids," p. 8.
45. Quoted in Naughton. "Literary Crusader Writes Stories About Real Kids," p. 8.
46. Quoted in Italie. "Walter Dean Myers, 73-Year-Old Author."
47. Italie. "Walter Dean Myers, 73-Year-Old Author."
48. Quoted in Italie. "Walter Dean Myers, 73-Year-Old Author."

49. Quoted in Mehren. "Fountain of Stories for Youth."
50. Quoted in National Public Radio. "To Do Well in Life, You Have to 'Read Well.'"
51. Quoted in Naughton. "Literary Crusader Writes Stories About Real Kids," p. 8.
52. Quoted in Learning First Alliance. "Prophet of Second Chances."
53. Quoted in National Public Radio. "A Writer and His Father, and 'a Barrier Between Us.'" *Morning Edition*, June 17, 2011. www.npr.org/2011/06/17/137223046/a-writer-and-his-father-and-a-barrier-between-us.
54. Quoted in StoryCorps. "He Never Said Anything Good About My Writing." Transcript of interview with Christopher Myers. http://storycorps.org/listen/stories/walter-myers-and-his-son-christopher-myers.
55. Myers. *Bad Boy*, p. 7.
56. Quoted in Reading Rockets. "Transcript of an Interview with Walter Dean Myers."

Chapter 5: From the Real to the Realer

57. Walter Dean Myers. *Fallen Angels*. New York: Scholastic, 1988, p. 321.
58. Snodgrass. *Walter Dean Myers*, p. 99.
59. Maria Salvadore. Review of *Fallen Angels* by Walter Dean Myers. *School Library Journal*, June–July 1988, p. 118.
60. Quoted in Marshall University Libraries. "Banned Book Week: *Fallen Angels*," August 6, 2010. www.marshall.edu/LIBRARY/bannedbooks/books/fallenangels.asp.
61. Quoted in Italie. "Walter Dean Myers, 73-Year-Old Author.
62. Quoted in American Booksellers Foundation for Free Expression. "Walter Dean Myers to Chair Children's Art Auction," May 3, 2012. www.abffe.org/?AuctionRelease2012.
63. Leonard S. Marcus. "Boys to Men." *New York Times*, May 11, 2008, p. 11. www.nytimes.com/2008/05/11/books/review/Marcus-t.html?pagewanted=print.
64. Paula Rohrlick. Review of *Sunrise over Fallujah*. *Kliatt*, May 2008, p. 15.

65. Quoted in *Something About the Author*. "Myers, Walter Dean," p. 155.

66. Quoted in *Something About the Author*. "Myers, Walter Dean," p. 155.

67. Quoted in Patty Campell. "The Sand in the Oyster: Radical Monster." A review of *Monster* by Walter Dean Myers. *Horn Book,* November/December 1999, p. 769.

68. Quoted in Hazel Rochman. "The *Booklist* Interview." *Booklist,* February 15, 2000, p. 1101.

69. Walter Dean Myers. "1994 Margaret A. Edwards Award Acceptance Speech," *Journal of Youth Services in Libraries,* Winter 1995, p. 132.

70. Roger Sutton. "*Monster.*" *Horn Book*, May/June 1999, p. 337.

71. Campell. "The Sand in the Oyster," p. 769.

72. Scholastic. "A Talk with Walter Dean Myers."

73. Quoted in Rochman. "The *Booklist* Interview," p. 1101.

74. Michael Didra. "Young Bookshelf." *Washington Post*, March 8, 1992, p. 11.

75. Bill Ott. Review of *The Greatest* by Walter Dean Myers. *Booklist*, January 1, 2002, p. 766.

76. *Publisher's Weekly*. Review of *At Her Majesty's Request*, March 22, 1999, p. 215.

Chapter 6: An Ambassador for Reading

77. Walter Dean Myers. *Handbook for Boys: A Novel*. New York: Harper-Collins, 2002, p. 86.

78. Walter Dean Myers. "And Then I Read . . . ," *Voices-from-the-Middle,* May 2001, pp. 58–61.

79. Walter Dean Myers. *The Beast*. New York: Scholastic 2003, p. 113.

80. Quoted in Authors on the Web. "YA Grows Up: 6 Best-selling Young Adult Authors Discuss the Most Misunderstood Genre." Interview with Laurie Halse Anderson, et al., 2001. The Book Report Network. Transcript, July 16, 2007.

81. Quoted in Adam Graham. "Author's Just a Kid at Heart." *Detroit News,* May 6, 2002.

82. Quoted in Reading Rockets. "Transcript of an interview with Walter Dean Myers."

83. Quoted in Cynthia Leitich Smith. "Co-Authors Interview: Walter Dean Myers & Ross Workman on *Kick*." *Cynsations* (blog), June 8, 2011. http://cynthialeitichsmith.blogspot .com/2011/06/co-authors-interview-walter-dean-myers .html.

84. Walter Dean Myers. "Walter Dean Myers." *Read*, February 25, 2005, p. 15.

85. Quoted in Dawn Morgan Elliott. "Interview with author Walter Dean Myers, Part II." WMNF 88.5FM Community Radio, September 29, 2010. www.wmnf.org/news_sto ries/8950.

86. Quoted in Learn First Alliance. "Prophet of Second Chances."

87. Walter Dean Myers. "Rescue the Children Along with the Bankers." *Huffington Post*, December 19, 2008. www .huffingtonpost.com/walter-dean-myers/rescue-the -children-along_b_152449.html.

88. Quoted in Bosman. "Children's Book Envoy Defines His Mission."

89. Bosman. "Children's Book Envoy Defines His Mission."

90. Quoted in Bosman. "Children's Book Envoy Defines His Mission."

1937

Walter Dean Myers is born Walter Milton Myers on August 12 to George Ambrose and Mary Green Myers in Martinsburg, West Virginia.

1940

Myers is placed in the foster care of Herbert and Florence Dean and raised in Harlem, New York, after his mother Mary dies during childbirth.

1942

Myers learns to read from comic books and Florence's *True Romance* magazines.

1945

Begins speech therapy while attending third grade at Public School 125.

1948

Publishes his first poem, "My Mother," in his fifth-grade yearbook; enrolls in the sixth grade, where his teacher encourages him to continue speech therapy and to pursue writing.

1952

Myers's foster father, Herbert, buys him his first typewriter.

1954

Drops out of Stuyvesant High School after finding out that his parents cannot afford to send him to college; he turns seventeen and joins the United States Army, where he becomes the star of his army basketball team.

1957

Completes his U.S. Army service and moves back to New York City where he begins working while attending night classes at City College.

1960

Marries first wife, Joyce Smith.

1961

First child, Karen, is born.

1963

Son Michael Dean is born.

1966

Begins work as an employment supervisor for the New York State Department of Labor.

1969

His first picture book, *Where Does the Day Go?*, wins a contest sponsored by the Council on Interracial Books for Children.

1970

Enrolls in a writing workshop at Columbia University taught by African American novelist and Harlem Writers Guild cofounder John O. Killens; accepts a job as senior trade book editor at Bobbs-Merrill publishing house; his first marriage ends in divorce.

1972

Publishes *The Dragon Takes a Wife* at Bobbs-Merrill and *The Dancers* at Parents Magazine Press; his foster mother, Florence, passes away.

1973

Marries Constance Brendel on June 19, 1973.

1974

Youngest son and future illustrator Christopher is born in Queens, New York.

1975

Publishes his first young-adult book, titled *Fast Sam, Cool Clyde, and Stuff* at Viking Press.

1977

Fired from his job as senior editor at Bobbs-Merrill; begins writing full-time for a living.

1981

Delacorte Press publishes *Hoops,* about a city teen's relationship with basketball; *Hoops* makes the American Library Association Notable Children's Books List and Best Books for Young Adults List and is runner-up for the Edgar Allan Poe Award.

1984

Receives his bachelor's degree from Empire State College.

1988

Scholastic Press publishes *Fallen Angels,* about young black soldiers in the Vietnam War.

1989

Fallen Angels wins the Coretta Scott King Award.

1992

Publishes *Now Is Your Time! The African American Struggle for Freedom* at HarperCollins, his first nonfiction book about African American life.

1993

Publishes *Malcolm X: By Any Means Necessary,* his second nonfiction book, on the life of civil rights activist Malcolm X; Myers's later nonfiction works concentrate on the contributions of African Americans in World War II, the American West, and Victorian England.

1994

Receives the Margaret A. Edwards Award, awarded by the Young Adult Library Services Association, for lifetime contribution to young-adult literature for *Hoops, Motown and Didi, Fallen Angels,* and *Scorpion.*

1997

Publishes *Harlem: A Poem* at Scholastic Press, celebrating Myers's old neighborhood; *Harlem* marks one of the first collaborations between Myers and his son Christopher, who illustrates it, and is awarded the Caldecott Honor Award.

1999

Publishes *Monster* at HarperCollins, about a Harlem teen's experience with robbery and murder; *Monster* is a finalist for the National Book Award.

2000

Monster is awarded the first Michael L. Printz Award for Excellence in Literature for Young Adults by the American Library Association.

2001

Publishes *Bad Boy*, a memoir about growing up in a tough and troubled city neighborhood; Myers is mentioned in Sharon Creech's poetic novella *Love That Dog,* published by HarperCollins.

2005

Publishes *Autobiography of My Dead Brother* at HarperCollins, about friendship in a violent neighborhood; *Autobiography of My Dead Brother* is a finalist for the National Book Award.

2008

Publishes *Sunrise Over Fallujah,* a sequel to *Fallen Angels* set in the Iraq War.

2009

Presents the May Hill Arbuthnot Honor Lecture by the American Library Association on April 19 at Clinton, Tennessee; daughter Karen passes away from complications due to AIDS.

2010

Awarded the Coretta Scott King–Virginia Hamilton Award for Lifetime Achievement on January 18; awarded the Chicago Tribune Young Adult Literary Prize on April 16.

2011

Publishes *We Are America: A Tribute from the Heart* at Harper-Collins, another collaboration with son Christopher.

2012

Named the third national Ambassador for Young People's Literature by the Center for the Book in the Library of Congress and Every Child a Reader of the Children's Book Council; hosts the American Booksellers Foundation for Free Expression (Mostly) Silent Children's Art Auction & Reception to Support Free Speech for Young People on June 6.

For More Information

Books

Rudie Sims Bishop. *Presenting Walter Dean Myers.* Ann Arbor: University of Michigan Press, 1990. Profiles the life of Walter Dean Myers, with close analyses of his important works.

Walter Dean Myers. *Bad Boy: A Memoir.* New York: HarperCollins, 2001. A memoir of Myers's life up to early adulthood, written in his own words.

Walter Dean Myers. *Handbook for Boys: A Novel.* New York: HarperCollins, 2002. A novel about two young friends who learn about life and redemption from working in a barbershop.

Walter Dean Myers. *Harlem.* New York: Scholastic, 1997. A celebration of Harlem told through images and song poems.

Walter Dean Myers. *Monster.* New York: HarperCollins, 1999. The story of sixteen-year-old Steve Harmon's murder trial told in screenplay and diary format.

Walter Dean Myers. *Sunrise Over Fallujah.* New York: Scholastic, 2008. A close-up of the Iraq War as told through the eyes of a young African American solider.

Emmanuel S. Nelson,ed. *Contemporary African American Novelists: A Bio-Bibliographical Critical Sourcebook.* Westport, CT: Greenwood, 1999. A critical sourcebook containing biographical information on Walter Dean Myers and many other influential African American Writers.

Mary Ellen Snodgrass. *Walter Dean Myers: A Literary Companion.* Jefferson, NC: McFarland, 2006. A brief literary analysis of books in Myers's bibliography, focusing on characters, dates, events, motifs, and background information on social and cultural references.

Periodicals

Patty Campell. "The Sand in the Oyster: Radical Monster." A review of *Monster* by Walter Dean Myers. *Horn Book*, November 1999.

R.D. Lane. "'Keepin' It Real': Walter Dean Myers and the Promise of African American Children's Literature." *African American Review*, Spring 1998.

Keith Miller, Allison Parker, and Walter Dean Myers. "Interview with Walter Dean Myers." *Journal of Adolescent & Adult Literacy*, May 2007.

Walter Dean Myers. "Writing for the Uninspired Reader." *English Journal*, January 2005.

Walter Dean Myers and Olubunmi Ishola. "An Interview with Walter Dean Myers." *World Literature Today*, May–June 2007.

Jim Naughton. "Literary Crusader Writes Stories About Real Kids." *Washington Post*, December 29, 1989.

Nathan Phillips. "Young Adult Literature: Monsters' Ink: How Walter Dean Myers Made Frankenstein Fun." *English Journal*, May 2003.

Internet Sources

Julie Bosman. "Children's Book Envoy Defines His Mission." *New York Times*. January 3, 2012. www.nytimes.com/2012/01/03 /books/walter-dean-myers-ambassador-for-young-peoples -literature.html?_r=1&pagewanted=all.

Jarrett Dapier. "Young Adult Realism."*In These Times,* May 9, 2011. www.inthesetimes.com/article/7283/young_adult _realism.

Hillel Italie. "Walter Dean Myers, 73-Year-Old Author, Beloved by Young Readers." *Huffington Post*, March 4, 2011. www .huffingtonpost.com/2011/03/04/walter-dean-myers -author_n_831559.html.

Learning First Alliance. "Prophet of Second Chances: A Conversation with Acclaimed Author Walter Dean Myers." *Public School Insights* (blog), January 31, 2009. www.learningfirst .org/node/2319.

Library of Congress. "National Ambassador for Young People's Literature Walter Dean Myers to Be Featured in Program for Young People," April 19, 2012. www.loc.gov/today /pr/2012/12-075.html.

Elizabeth Mehren. "Fountain of Stories for Youth." *Los Angeles Times*, October 15, 1997. http://articles.latimes.com/1997 /oct/15/news/ls-42828.

National Public Radio. "To Do Well in Life, You Have to 'Read Well.'" *Morning Edition*, January 10, 2012. www.npr.org/2012/01/10/144944598/to-do-well-in-life-you-have-to-read-well.

Clem Richardson. "Author's Message to Youth: Read, Graduate, Go to College." *New York Daily News,* January 19, 2012. http://articles.nydailynews.com/2012-0119/news/30644952_1_eighth-graders-walter-dean-myers-proficient-readers.

Kay E. Vandergrift. "Learning About Walter Dean Myers." Rutgers University, May 10, 1996. http://comminfo.rutgers.edu/professional-development/childlit/myers.html.

Debra Lau Whelan. "Dynamic Duo: Myers Teams Up with Teen Author." *School Library Journal.* January 24, 2011. www.schoollibraryjournal.com/slj/newslettersnewsletterbucketextrahelping2/888897477/dynamic_duo_myers_teams_up.html.csp.

Websites

Harlem Writers Guild (http://theharlemwritersguild.org). Information on the organization that sparked Walter Dean Myers's writing career.

HarperCollins Author Website (www.harpercollins.com/authors/12522/Walter_Dean_Myers/index.aspx). Contains essays, interviews, and reading guides on Myers's work.

Second Chance Initiative (www.adlit.org/second_chances). Contains podcasts, video interviews with the author, lesson plans, and reading guides centered around Myers's *Dope Sick.*

Walter Dean Myers's Website (www.walterdeanmyers.net). The author's website contains reviews, a full bibliography, and a brief bio.

Who Is America (www.who-is-america.com). Contains videos inspired by Walter Dean and Christopher Myers's collaboration *We Are America*, a celebration of the nation and its diversity.

A

Amistad affair (1839), 64

"And Then I Read . . . "
(Walter Dean Myers), 68

Army life, 23–24

At Her Majesty's Request
(Walter Dean Myers), 65

Awards, 8, 39, 46, 49, 57,
67

B

Bad Boy (Walter Dean
Myers), 8–9, 12, 54, 55–
56, 58, 65–66

Baldwin, James, 20–21, *21*

The Beast (Walter Dean
Myers), 68–69

Beat Generation, 26

Biographies, 64–65

Birth, 10

Brendel, Constance (wife),
32, 38, 43

C

Characters, 35, 47–48
historical figures as, 64
male, 49

Childhood, 7–8, 11–12

Children's books, race in,
30

Coleridge, Samuel Taylor,
24

Columbine High School
shooting (1999), 66

Coretta Scott King Award,
39

Council on Interracial
Books for Children, 27,
30

D

The Dancers (Walter Dean
Myers), 31, 42

Dean, Florence (step
mother), 10, 11, 15, 16,
33

Dean, Herbert Julius
(father), 10, 11, 15, 50,
52

Detroit, 70

Divorce, 27

Dope Sick (Walter Dean
Myers), 69

The Dragon Takes a Wife
(Walter Dean Myers), 6,
31, 42

F

Fallen Angels (Walter Dean
Myers), 55–57, 67
bans on, 75

Fast Sam, Cool Clyde, and Stuff (Walter Dean Myers), 35, 44

Fly, Jimmy, Fly! (Walter Dean Myers), 33, 42

G

Game (Walter Dean Myers), 58

Ginsberg, Alan, 26

Giovanni, Nikki, 34, *34*

The Glory Field (Walter Dean Myers), 41–42

H

Handbook for Boys (Walter Dean Myers), 67–68

Harlem, 54

of 1940s, 14, 17

Harlem Summer (Walter Dean Myers), 41

Harlem Writers Guild, 26, 27

Harris, Eric, 66

Hoops (Walter Dean Myers), 46, 47, 58

bans on, 75

Hurston, Zora Neale, 53

I

Incarceration rates, in U.S., 59

It Ain't All for Nothing (Walter Dean Myers), 45–46

J

Juvenile detention centers, 39, 50, 61, 72

K

Kerouac, Jack, 26, *26*

Kick (Walter Dean Myers and Ross Workman), 71

Kids' Right to Read Project and American Booksellers Foundation for Free Expression (ABFFE), 58

Killens, John O., 26–27

Klebold, Dylan, 66

L

Langston Hughes Children's Literature Festival, 72

Lasher, Irwin, 14

The Legend of Tarik (Walter Dean Myers), 40, 51

L'Ouverture, Toussaint, 64

M

Malcolm X, *65*

Malcolm X: By Any Means Necessary (Walter Dean Myers), 64

Marriage, 25, 32

Martin, Kevin, 68

Mojo and the Russians (Walter Dean Myers), 36, 44

Monster (Walter Dean Myers), 54, 62, *62*, 75

Muhammad, Ali, 64
Myers, Christopher (son), 39, 43, *53*
  as illustrator for father's books, 53, 54
Myers, Karen (daughter), 25
Myers, Michael (son), 25, 58–59
Myers, Sonny (brother), 55, 56
Myers, Walter Dean, 23, *28, 41, 52, 74*
  as book editor, 29, 31, 34, 36
  at book signings, *33, 45*
  as boy, *13*
  mission of, 44
  as national ambassador for young people's literature, 67, 76
  with son Christopher, *53*
  sources of inspiration for, 38–39
  speech impediment of, 11–12, *28*

N
Now Is Your Time! (Walter Dean Myers), 64

O
The Outside Shot (Walter Dean Myers), 67

P
Prison, research, 59–61

Prison writing workshops, 73

R
The Righteous Revenge of Artemis Bonner (Walter Dean Myers), 51

S
Science fiction, 51
Second Chance Initiative, 69
Shadow of the Red Moon (Walter Dean Myers), 51, *54*
Shooter (Walter Dean Myers), 63
Smith, Joyce (wife), 25, 27
Snodgrass, Mary Ellen, 35
Sonny's Blues (Baldwin), 20, 21
Sportswriting, 58
Stuyvesant High School, *14,* 14–15
Sunrise Over Fallujah (Walter Dean Myers), 59, *60*

T
Themes, 46, 55, 58
  black urban life, 46–49
  bullying, 63
  prisoners/juvenile offenders, reading, 67–69

V
Vietnam Veterans
  Memorial (Washington,
  D.C.), 56

W
Wall of Respect (Chicago),
  29
Walter Dean Myers
  Publishing Institute, 72
Walter Dean Myers
  (Snodgrass), 35

Wasserman, Harriet, 33
Where Does the Day Go?
  (Walter Dean Myers), 6,
  27, 30
Won't Know Until I Get There
  (Walter Dean Myers), 46
Workman, Ross, 70–71
Writing process, 39–43

Y
Young Landlords (Walter
  Dean Myers), 39, 46

About the Author

Elizabeth Hoover is a writer based in Harrisonburg, Virginia, where she writes about art, music, and books for a variety of publications. You can see more of her work at www.ehooverink.com.